J.K. LASSER'S™

TAX
SAVINGS IN YOUR
POCKET

Look for these and other titles from J.K. Lasser™—Practical Guides for All Your Financial Needs

J.K. Lasser's Pick Winning Stocks by Edward F. Mrkvicka, Jr.

J.K. Lasser's Invest Online by LauraMaery Gold and Dan Post

J.K. Lasser's Year-Round Tax Strategies by David S. DeJong and Ann Gray Jakabcin

J.K. Lasser's Taxes Made Easy for Your Home-Based Business by Gary W. Carter

J.K. Lasser's Finance and Tax for Your Family Business by Barbara Weltman

J.K. Lasser's Pick Winning Mutual Funds by Jerry Tweddell with Jack Pierce

J.K. Lasser's Your Winning Retirement Plan by Henry K. Hebeler

J.K. Lasser's Winning with Your 401(k) by Grace Weinstein

J.K. Lasser's Winning with Your 403(b) by Pam Horowitz

J.K. Lasser's Strategic Investing after 50 by Julie Jason

J.K. Lasser's Winning Financial Strategies for Women by Rhonda Ecker and Denise Gustin-Piazza

J.K. Lasser's Online Taxes by Barbara Weltman

J.K. Lasser's Pick Stocks Like Warren Buffett by Warren Boroson

J.K. Lasser's New Tax Law Simplified

J.K. Lasser's New Rules for Retirement and Tax by Paul Westbrook

J.K. Lasser's New Rules for Small Business Taxes by Barbara Weltman

J.K. Lasser's Investor's Tax Guide by Elaine Floyd

J.K. Lasser's Choosing the Right Long-Term Care Insurance by Ben Lipson

J.K. Lasser's Winning Ways to Save for College by Barbara Wagner

J.K. Lasser's Financial Basics for Business Managers by John Tracy

J.K. LASSER'S™

TAX SAVINGS IN YOUR POCKET

YOUR GUIDE TO THE NEW TAX LAWS

Barbara Weltman, Esq.

John Wiley & Sons, Inc.

For general information on our other products and services, or technical
support, please contact our Customer Care Department within the
United States at 800-762-2974, outside the United States at 317-572-3993
or fax 317-572-4002.

Wiley also publishes its books in a variety of electronic formats. Some
content that appears in print may not be available in electronic books.

Library of Congress Cataloging-in-Publication Data:

ISBN 0-471-22726-9

Printed in the United States of America.

10   9   8   7   6   5   4   3   2   1

Contents

Introduction

The tax law is constantly changing, and the laws surrounding your 2002 tax return are no exception. For example, within just a nine-month period Congress enacted three major tax packages:

1. The Economic Growth and Tax Relief Reconciliation Act of 2001, signed into law on June 7, 2001, the largest tax cut bill in 20 years ($1.35 trillion), makes over 400 changes in income, estate, and gift tax rules.

2. The Victims of Terrorism Tax Relief Act of 2001, signed into law on January 23, 2002, provides significant tax assistance to military personnel, victims of terrorism, and their families.

3. The Job Creation and Worker Assistance Act of 2002, signed into law on March 9, 2002, is a $38.7 billion stimulus package providing not only funds for 13 additional weeks of unemployment benefits but also numerous tax breaks for small business and individuals.

Note that 2002 is the first year that many of the provisions created by these and other laws start to take effect. The new rules provide important tax-saving opportunities for individuals in 2002 and in years to come. Generally, the new rules provide incentives in such areas as:

- Building up retirement savings.
- Saving and paying for college.
- Investing in capital equipment and hiring new workers for business.

It is imperative that you are prepared to take advantage of every opportunity available to you. With the stock market in flux, it is now more important than ever to watch over your tax expenses.

The changes in the tax laws aren't limited to income taxes; they extend to estate, gift, and generation-skipping transfer taxes as well. Changes in these laws allow you to transfer more of your property to others on a tax-free basis—during your lifetime or at death—enabling your family and others to keep more of the assets you've amassed.

These new laws aren't the only changes affecting tax planning for 2002 and 2003. Cost-of-living adjustments to various deductions and credits, important court decisions, key Treasury regulations and IRS pronouncements, as well as law changes enacted in earlier years that take effect now all have an impact on your taxes this year. These changes combine to make tax planning complex and challenging— but most of all rewarding in the tax savings you can realize if you know what to do.

You don't have to be a tax professional to learn which new rules to take advantage of and how to go about it. All you need is an understanding of what the new rules are, including their eligibility requirements. Then you can decide which changes fit your situation and lifestyle so you can make the most of the tax-saving opportunities available.

This book is designed to acquaint you with the income tax changes affecting your 2002 returns as well as the changes in estate, gift, and generation-skipping transfer taxes taking effect in 2002. It also highlights when you need to file amended returns in order to benefit from law changes to prior years. And it points out new rules that will take effect in 2003 or later years so that you can adopt comprehensive strategies to save you tax dollars not only in 2002 but in the coming years as well.

J.K. LASSER'S™

TAX SAVINGS IN YOUR POCKET

CHAPTER 1

Income Tax Rate Reductions

Our federal income tax rate structure uses graduated tax rates to impose a higher rate of tax as your income rises. For higher-income taxpayers, the new law changes provide some rate reduction relief (low- and moderate-income taxpayers do not experience any rate relief at this time).

This chapter explains how the income tax rates decline for 2002 and what you can do to take advantage of the changes. You will also learn about the multiple capital gains tax rates in effect for 2002. And you will find out about the alternative minimum tax (AMT)—what it is, whether it applies to you, the changes for 2002, and what you can do to avoid or reduce this tax.

General income-shifting strategies are provided to enable

you to redistribute wealth within your family in order to save income taxes. Finally, special coverage is given to adjusted gross income (AGI)—the measuring rod for determining eligibility for many of the tax breaks discussed throughout this book—and what you can do to control your AGI in order to increase your eligibility for these tax opportunities.

Income Tax Rates

For 2002, you'll probably pay less income tax than you would have paid in 2001 (if your income is about the same in both years). The simple reason is that the federal income tax rates are lower in 2002. But the complete reason is more complex.

For 2002, there are six individual federal income tax brackets: 10 percent, 15 percent, 27 percent, 30 percent, 35 percent, and 38.6 percent. The two lowest tax brackets (10 percent and 15 percent) are the same as they were in 2001—they are unchanged by the new law. The four highest tax brackets, however, have each been reduced by one-half of one percentage point (they were 27.5 percent, 30.5 percent, 35.5 percent and 39.1 percent respectively in 2001).

Unlike 2001, there is no rebate check for the 10 percent bracket. The lowest tax bracket is, however, reflected in the 2002 tables that employers use to figure income tax withholding on wages to employees, so if you're subject to wage withholding, the benefit from the 10 percent rate has been taken into account throughout the year.

In addition to a reduction in rates, all of the tax brackets *except* the 10 percent bracket have been adjusted for inflation. So you can earn more income in 2002 without being pushed into a higher tax bracket. (See Example 1.)

The complete tax brackets for all filers in 2002 are outlined in Tables 1.1 to 1.4.

Tax Planning

Any tax planning you undertake depends on your personal situation. However, the following generalities provide some guidance for taking advantage of changes in the tax rates.

INCOME DEFERRAL. Shifting income from the current year into a future year saves you money because it postpones the time in which you pay

LOOKING AHEAD

There is no additional reduction in the tax rates for 2003. However, all of the tax brackets except the 10 percent bracket will again be adjusted for inflation. The adjustment in the tax brackets for married persons filing jointly to provide relief from the so-called "marriage penalty" is discussed in Chapter 2.

Example 1

In 2001, the 15 percent tax bracket for singles applied to taxable income up to $27,050. In 2002, the same tax bracket for singles applies to taxable income up to $27,950. This means that you can have $900 more income in 2002 than in 2001 and still remain in the same tax bracket.

TABLE 1.1 2002 Tax Rate Schedule—Single

If Taxable Income Is: Over—	But Not Over—	The Tax Is:	Of the Amount Over—
$ 0	$ 6,000	10%	$ 0
6,000	27,950	$ 600.00 + 15%	6,000
27,950	67,700	3,892.50 + 27%	27,950
67,700	141,250	14,625.00 + 30%	67,700
141,250	307,050	36,690.00 + 35%	141,250
307,050		94,720.00 + 38.6%	307,050

TABLE 1.2 2002 Tax Rate Schedule—Head of Household

If Taxable Income Is: Over—	But Not Over—	The Tax Is:	Of the Amount Over—
$ 0	$ 10,000	10%	$ 0
10,000	37,450	$ 1,000.00 + 15%	10,000
37,450	96,700	5,117.50 + 27%	37,450
96,700	156,600	21,115.00 + 30%	96,700
156,600	307,050	39,085.00 + 35%	156,600
307,050		91,742.50 + 38.6%	307,050

TABLE 1.3 Tax Rate Schedule—Married Filing Jointly or Qualifying Widow(er)

If Taxable Income Is: Over—	But Not Over—	The Tax Is:	Of the Amount Over—
$ 0	$ 12,000	10%	$ 0
12,000	46,700	$ 1,200.00 + 15%	12,000
46,700	112,850	6,405.00 + 27%	46,700
112,850	171,950	24,265.50 + 30%	112,850
171,950	307,050	41,995.50 + 35%	171,950
307,050		89,280.50 + 38.6%	307,050

TABLE 1.4 2002 Tax Rate Schedule—Married Filing Separately

If Taxable Income Is: Over—	But Not Over—	The Tax Is:	Of the Amount Over—
$ 0	$ 6,000	10%	$ 0
6,000	23,350	$ 600.00 + 15%	6,000
23,350	56,425	3,202.50 + 27%	23,350
56,425	85,975	12,132.75 + 30%	56,425
85,975	153,525	20,997.75 + 35%	85,975
153,525		44,640.25 + 38.6%	153,525

the tax on the income. For example, if you receive income in December 2002, you owe the tax on that income by April 15, 2003. But if you defer that income for one month—to January 2003—you don't owe the tax until April 15, 2004.

But tax postponement isn't the main incentive for income deferral. Because of cost-of-living adjustments to the 15 percent, 27 percent, 30 percent, 35 percent, and 38.6 percent tax brackets, income shifted from 2002 into 2003 may be taxed at a lower rate. This translates into a real tax savings. Whether income deferral produces this result depends on whether that income falls into a lower tax bracket. (See Example 2.)

How do you defer income into a later year? There are several proven strategies you can use to shift income from 2002 into 2003.

Example 2

You have $500 in income that you can shift to 2003 instead of realizing it in 2002. Assume that if you had received it in 2002, it would have exceeded the limit for the 15 percent bracket and so would have fallen into the 27 percent bracket. But because you receive the income in 2003 it is still in the 15 percent bracket because of adjustments made to the bracket that allow more income to be received at that rate. So instead of paying $135 tax on the $500 income ($500 × 27%), you pay only $75 tax on that same income ($500 × 15%), a $60 tax savings.

- Make investments that pay income after December 31, 2002. For example, after June 30 you invest in a six-month certificate of deposit coming due after the end of the year. Interest is not considered to have been received on this CD until 2003. Similar results can be obtained with three-month and six-month Treasury bills that come due after the end of 2002.

- Self-employed individuals on the cash method of reporting their income and expenses can delay year-end billing so that accounts receivable for work performed in 2002 or goods sold in 2002 will be paid in 2003. Of course this deferral strategy is *not* advisable where there is any concern about collecting the accounts receivable—in such a case it's better to bill and collect as soon as possible.

Longer deferral may prove even more advantageous because the tax rates above the 15 percent bracket are scheduled to decline again in 2004 and again in 2006. So income shifted from 2002 into these later years may be taxed at even lower rates, irrespective of cost-of-living adjustments that will continue to be made. There are also several reliable strategies you can use to defer income from 2002 until several years into the future.

- Make contributions to tax-deferred accounts such as 401(k) plans, 403(b) annuities, 457 plans, deductible individual retirement accounts (IRAs), and commercial annuities. You may find yourself in a lower tax bracket when funds are withdrawn later on than you are now.

- Arrange for deferred compensation. Your employer may be willing to defer the payment of a year-end bonus or a percentage of your salary until you leave the company (typically upon retirement). Again, at that time you may find yourself in a lower tax bracket than you are in 2002. Generally, the deferred compensation arrangement must be entered into *before* the income is earned.

Caution

You can't shift income merely by refusing to accept it in 2002. Under a tax rule called "constructive receipt," if you have the right to income in 2002, it's yours even if you don't accept it. For example, if you receive a check at the end of December it's income to you even though you don't cash or deposit it until January. And you risk collection of the deferred compensation down the road since the funds remain subject to the claims of the company's creditors (if they are secured then you are treated as being in constructive receipt of them).

DEDUCTION ACCELERATION. The flip side to deferring income is accelerating deductions into 2002 that might otherwise be taken in 2003 if you expect to be in a lower tax bracket in 2003 than in 2002. This is because deductions are worth more as tax brackets are higher. (See Example 3.)

Example 3

You itemize deductions and plan to make a $100 charitable contribution in 2003. Should you make it in 2002 instead? Assume that in 2002 you're in the 27 percent tax bracket but in 2003 expect to be in the 15 percent tax bracket because your income will remain constant while the tax bracket adjusts to allow more income to be received at the lower rate. Your $100 deduction made in 2002 saves you $27; in 2003, in contrast, it will produce only a $15 tax savings.

Here are some strategies you can use to accelerate into 2002 deductions you might otherwise have taken in 2003:

- Make discretionary expenditures—elective medical procedures that are not reimbursed by insurance and which are deductible (e.g., additional prescription sunglasses) and charitable contributions. For instance, if you've pledged this year to contribute $1,000 a year for five years to your alma mater, you may wish to satisfy that pledge in full in 2002 when the deduction for this charitable contribution is worth more than if you fulfill the pledge in 2003, 2004, 2005, and 2006.

- Prepay state and local income and real estate taxes. For example, state and local tax payments due in January 2003 can be paid in December 2002 so they become deductible in 2002. *Be careful:* Don't prepay these taxes if you're subject to the alternative minimum tax

(AMT) (explained later in this chapter); you can't deduct these taxes for AMT so you lose the tax benefit of the prepayment.

- If you have a self-employed business on the cash method of accounting, prepay certain expenses that can be deducted this year. For instance, stock up on supplies and pay off all outstanding bills for deductible items before the end of the year. *Be careful:* Don't prepay multiyear items (e.g., three-year subscriptions or multiyear insurance premiums) since they are deductible only over the period to which they relate.

Capital Gains Rates

The capital gains tax rates have *not* been changed in any way for 2002. There are still about a dozen different capital gains rates to contend with. The applicable rate can depend on the type of assets you own, how long you've held them, and the income tax bracket you're in for the year in which you sell the assets.

IF YOU'RE IN THE 10 PERCENT OR 15 PERCENT TAX BRACKET. The general rate on long-term capital gains—gains from the disposition of capital assets held more than one year—is 10 percent. For assets held more than five years, the rate drops to just 8 percent. These rates apply regardless of the type of capital asset involved. (See Example 4.)

Example 4

On November 1, 2002, you sell stock you acquired on May 1, 1995, for a gain of $1,000. You are in the 15 percent tax bracket on your ordinary income. Your gain is taxed at a rate of 8 percent. But if you acquired the stock on May 1, 2000, you'd pay 10 percent on the gain—you owned the stock more than one year but not more than five years.

IF YOU'RE IN A TAX BRACKET ABOVE 15 PERCENT. The general rate on long-term capital gains is 20 percent (including assets held more than five years). (See Example 5.)

For those in tax brackets above the 15 percent rate, there are other capital gains rates that may apply. These include:

- The 25 percent rate on unrecaptured depreciation. This is all of straight-line depreciation on real estate other than a principal residence and all straight-line depreciation after May 6, 1987, on a principal resi-

Example 5

Same facts as in Example 4 except you are in the 27 percent tax bracket on your ordinary income. Your gain is taxed at 20 percent—whether you acquired the stock on May 1, 1995, or on May 1, 2000.

dence (for example, on the portion of a residence used as a home office).

- The 28 percent rate on collectibles gains and gains on certain small business stock (called Section 1202 gains). However, those in the 27 percent tax bracket may pay only 27 percent, not 28 percent, on these gains.

- The 18 percent rate on gains from assets acquired after December 31, 2000, and held more than five years. This rate also applies to assets held at the start of 2001 for which you elected on your 2001 return to report as a "deemed sale." You reported the gain to January 1, 2001 (January 2, 2001, in the case of publicly traded securities) that would have resulted had you actually sold the asset and revised your tax cost basis and holding period to reflect this action. Whether you have new assets or assets reported as a deemed sale, the five-year post-2000 holding period means that the low rate does not come into use until 2006.

Alternative Minimum Tax Rates

The alternative minimum tax (AMT) is a shadow tax system designed to ensure that all individuals with income above a certain amount—even those with substantial write-offs (other than tax credits)—pay at least some federal income tax. Unlike the tax brackets for the regular income tax, the two AMT rates of 26 percent and 28 percent are not indexed annually for inflation.

EXEMPTION AMOUNT. Only alternative minimum taxable in-come—your taxable income for regular tax purposes ad-justed by special tax preferences and other adjustment items—above a certain amount is subject to the AMT. This threshold is determined by your AMT exemption amount. The AMT exemption amount (increased in 2001) remains unchanged for 2002. (See Table 1.5.) (The in-crease to the exemption amount is temporary and applies only through 2004.)

For a child under age 14 who is subject to the kiddie tax on unearned income, there is a special AMT exemption. This exemption is higher in 2002 than it was in 2001. The child's AMT exemption amount in 2002 is limited to $5,500 plus any earned income. However, the child's AMT exemp-tion amount cannot exceed the exemption amount for a sin-gle individual—$35,750.

TAX CREDITS. Even if you do wind up with a tentative AMT li-ability, you may not have to pay it. This liability can be off-set by certain tax credits. The earned income credit is no longer reduced by the alternative minimum tax. Also, per-sonal tax credits (e.g., the child tax credit, education cred-

TABLE 1.5 AMT Exemption Amounts

Filing Status	AMT Exemption
Single and head of household	$35,750
Married filing jointly and surviving spouse	49,000
Married filing separately	24,500

its, the dependent care credit, and the adoption credit) can be used to offset both the regular tax and the AMT. As in the past, AMT liability may also be offset by the foreign tax credit.

AMT Planning

In order to plan effectively to minimize or avoid the AMT, you must understand how this alternative tax system works. Certain write-offs allowed for regular tax purposes can't be used in figuring AMT. And certain income items that were not subject to regular tax are now taxable for AMT purposes.

LOOKING AHEAD

After 2003, the use of personal credits (other than the foreign tax credit) to offset AMT is restricted to the child tax credit and the adoption credit. This means that unless Congress takes further action, you lose the benefit of your other tax credits to the extent you are subject to the AMT.

DEDUCTION PLANNING. For AMT purposes, no deduction is allowed for state and local income taxes. This means that accelerating state and local income tax payments to boost regular tax deductions for the year may prove meaningless if it triggers or increases AMT. Before making any year-end payments of state and local income or property taxes otherwise due in January of next year, consider the impact that this prepayment will have on AMT.

For AMT purposes, no deduction is allowed for miscellaneous itemized deductions. If you have substantial legal expenses, unreimbursed employee business expenses, investment expenses, or other miscellaneous expenses, you lose the benefit of their deduction for regular tax purposes if it they trigger or increase AMT. To avoid this result, it may be helpful to minimize your miscellaneous deductions.

- When retaining an attorney for a legal action involving a contingency fee, be sure that the arrangement creates an interest for the attorney in the recovery so that you need only report any net recovery (the amount you receive after the attorney receives his or her share). If you do not, or if state law does not create such an interest, then you must report the recovery in full and claim any legal fees as a miscellaneous itemized deduction for regular income tax purposes (but not for AMT purposes).

- Request that your employer use an accountable plan to cover employee business expenses. Under an accountable plan, employer advances or reimbursements for travel and entertainment costs are not treated as income to you; you must substantiate your business expenses to your employer and return any excess reimbursements. In contrast, if your employer has a nonaccountable plan, employer reimbursements for your business expenses are treated as additional income to you. Then you can deduct your business expenses, but only as a miscellaneous itemized deduction. Such expenses become deductible only to the extent that the total exceeds 2 percent of your adjusted gross income. And this itemized deduction is *not* allowable for alternative minimum tax (AMT) purposes, which may result in triggering or increasing AMT.

Another write-off for regular tax purposes that can't be claimed for AMT purposes is the deduction for personal exemptions. It may be advisable in appropriate circumstances to waive the dependency exemption. Since personal exemptions are not deductible for AMT purposes, even middle-income taxpayers with a substantial number of dependents may fall victim to the AMT. (See Example 6.)

INCENTIVE STOCK OPTION PLANNING. If you hold incentive stock options (ISOs), which give you the right to buy a set number of shares of your employer's stock at a set price within a set time, exercising them does not produce any income for regular tax purposes. But the spread between the option price and stock price on the date the ISOs are exercised is an adjustment to alternative minimum taxable income. In effect, even though the exercise of ISOs does not produce any regular income tax consequences, such action may trigger AMT. Thus, it is important to time carefully the exercise of ISOs to avoid the AMT.

Example 6

You and your siblings all contribute to the support of your elderly parent. If you may be subject to the AMT but your siblings are not, let one of them claim the exemption under a multiple support agreement. Forgoing the dependency exemption for regular tax purposes ($3,000 in 2002) may mean avoiding or reducing your AMT exposure.

Generally it is advisable to spread the exercise of ISOs over a number of years rather than exercising them all at once. This will minimize any adverse tax impact.

But tax considerations may have to take a backseat to other factors. Watch out for expiration dates on the options. Also consider moves in the stock prices and the availability of cash to exercise the options.

Income Shifting

One intrafamily tax-saving strategy is to shift income from someone in a higher tax bracket to someone in a lower tax bracket. In this way, the income remains in the family but the tax bite is reduced. In the past, when top tax rates were higher, the tax savings from income shifting were more dramatic. But even with today's reduced tax rates, there can still be considerable tax savings for the family. (See Example 7.)

Example 7

In 2002, parents in the 35 percent tax bracket give property worth $22,000 to their teenager who is in the 10 percent tax bracket. Assuming the property yields ordinary income of $2,000, the tax would be only $200 ($2,000 × 10%) for the teenager. If the parents had kept the property, they would have paid $700 ($2,000 × 35%). The transfer keeps the $2,000 in the family but saves it $500 in taxes ($700 − $200).

Income shifting can also produce substantial savings if capital gains producing property can be shifted from a family member in a higher tax bracket to one in a lower bracket. (See Example 8.)

Strategies for Income Shifting

Income can be shifted from a higher tax bracket family member to one in a lower bracket by giving income-producing property. (The rules on making tax-free gifts in 2002 are discussed in Chapter 4.) Here are some types of property to consider giving away for income-shifting purposes:

- Cash that can be invested in income-producing property.
- Dividend-paying stocks.
- Corporate bonds and Treasury securities.

Example 8

In 2002, parents in the 35 percent tax bracket give property worth $22,000 (for which they paid $10,000 six years ago) to their teenager, who is in the 10 percent tax bracket. If the teenager sells the asset in 2002, he would pay a capital gains tax of $960 ($12,000 × 8%). (The parents' basis in and holding period for the asset carry over to the teenager when the gift is made.) If the parents sell the property, they would owe a capital gains tax of $2,400 ($12,000 × 20%). The transfer keeps the $12,000 profit in the family but saves it $1,440 in taxes ($2,400 − $960).

- Stock and shares in mutual funds with unrealized capital gain.
- Interests in an S corporation, limited liability company, or partnership owned by the parent or grandparent. Doing so means that the child's share of the entity's income passes through to the child and is taxed at the child's lower tax rate.

Caution

It is generally not advisable to shift income to a child under the age of 14 because of the kiddie tax. The child's unearned income (e.g., dividends on stock, interest on a bank account, or capital gains distributions from mutual funds) over $1,500 in 2002 is taxed to the child at the parent's highest marginal tax rate.

BASIS. Remember that when property is gifted, the recipient generally takes over the same tax basis and holding period as the donor. The precise rules on basis depend on whether the recipient sells the property at a gain or a loss and whether you paid any gift tax when you made the gift.

- *Sale at a gain.* Basis is the same as in the hands of the donor (but not more than the value of the property at the time of the gift), plus any gift tax paid by the donor.
- *Sale at a loss.* Basis is the lower of the donor's basis or the value of the gift at the time it was made. (See Examples 9 and 10.)

Example 9

You paid $1,000 for property on May 1, 1992, and give it to your teenager on May 1, 2002. At the time of the gift the property is worth $1,200. A month later your child sells it for $1,300. Your child's basis for determining the gain is $1,000 (the same as yours) and your child's holding period starts on May 1, 1992 (the same as yours).

Example 10

Same facts as in Example 9 except that at the time of the gift the value of the property had declined to $900 and the child sells it in 2003 when the value of the property has declined still further to $500. In this instance, the child's basis is $900, which is less than your basis of $1,000.

Adjusted Gross Income

Adjusted gross income is more than a line on your tax return. It is a figure that's used to determine whether you are eligible for more than two dozen tax benefits—many of which are discussed throughout this book. These include:

- A $25,000 rental loss allowance.
- The portion of Social Security benefits included in income.

- An exclusion for interest on U.S. savings bonds used to pay higher education costs and an exclusion for employer-paid adoption expenses.

- Eligibility to make contributions to Coverdell education savings accounts, Roth IRAs, and deductible IRA contributions if an active plan participant.

- Eligibility to convert traditional IRAs to Roth IRAs.

- Above-the-line deductions for college tuition and student loan interest.

- A reduction in personal exemptions.

- An ability to claim itemized deductions—medical expenses, charitable contributions, casualty and theft losses, miscellaneous itemized expenses.

- A limit on itemized deductions.

- An ability to claim credits—child tax credit, dependent care credit, Hope and lifetime learning credits, earned income credit, credit for the elderly and disabled, adoption credit, health care credit, and credit for retirement savings contributions.

- Determining which estimated tax safe harbor rule to rely upon.

MODIFIED ADJUSTED GROSS INCOME (MAGI). In some cases, you can't simply look at the line on your tax return labeled "adjusted gross income" (line 35 of the 2002 Form 1040) to find the correct AGI limit—you must adjust your AGI by certain items. These items vary with the tax benefit involved. Typically, AGI is modified by ignoring certain exclusions (such as the exclusions for foreign earned income and savings bond interest used to pay higher education costs) to arrive at modified adjusted gross income (MAGI).

STRATEGIES FOR CONTROLLING AGI. Generally you aim to keep your AGI down so you are eligible to claim various tax write-offs or other benefits. In limited situations you may want to *increase* your AGI for certain purposes (such as to claim greater charitable contribution deductions). Here are some ways to achieve your objectives of decreasing (or increasing) AGI.

- *Using salary reduction options to decrease AGI.* To the extent you reduce your income, your AGI is lower. You can so do without forgoing earnings by taking advantage of various salary reduction arrangements you may be offered. These include making contributions to 401(k) plans, 403(b) annuities, and SIMPLE plans (savings incentive match plans for employees) and contributing to flexible spending arrangements (FSAs) to pay for medical and dependent care expenses on a pretax basis. The amounts you contribute to salary reduction arrangements are *not* treated as current income—they are not included in your W-2 pay—so your AGI is lower even though you obtain a tax benefit from your earnings (retirement savings, selection of benefit options, etc.).

- *Investing for tax-free or tax-deferred income to decrease AGI.* To the extent you can avoid reporting income this year you can keep your AGI down. Consider investing in tax-free bonds or tax-free bond funds if you are in a tax bracket above 27 percent. Also consider deferral-type investments—U.S. savings bonds and annuities—where income from earnings on the investments is not reported until a future year. Switch from dividend-paying stocks to growth stocks to eliminate current income while attaining appreciation that will be reported as capital gains later on.

- *Selling on an installment basis or making a tax-free exchange to decrease AGI.* An installment sale spreads your income over the term you set so that your income won't spike in the year of the sale. Or defer the gain by making a tax-free exchange of investment or business property; any gain realized on the initial exchange is postponed until the property acquired in the exchange is later disposed of.

- *Using year-end strategies to decrease AGI.* Defer income as explained earlier in this chapter to minimize your AGI for the current year. ***Important:*** Increasing your itemized deductions, such as deductions for medical expenses or charitable contributions, by accelerating discretionary payments won't cut your AGI (itemized deductions are taken into account *after* you figure your AGI).

- *Taking advantage of above-the-line deductions to decrease AGI.* Make full use of the $3,000 capital loss write-off against ordinary income; make sure that you realize any investment losses before the end of the year to do so while enabling you to reposition your holdings. Learn about new write-offs (e.g., new deductions for an educator's out-of-pocket expenses or college tuition explained in Chapter 2).

- *Reporting a child's income on your return to increase AGI.* If you have a child under age 14 whose only income for 2002 is less than $7,500, all of which is from interest, dividends, or capital gains distributions, you can elect to report the child's income on your return. Generally, this election is *not* advisable because it increases your AGI, thereby limiting your eligibility for many tax items. But in some cases, the election not only saves you the time and money of preparing a child's separate return, but also enables you to achieve some benefits. For example, you may be able to boost your investment interest deduction by adding your child's investment income to your own. Or you may be able to claim a larger charitable contribution deduction by increasing your AGI.

CHAPTER 2

Tax Relief for Families

The tax law provides important tax breaks for families— in the form of various exclusions, deductions, and credits. Families are not limited to the old notion of two parents with 2.3 children—for tax purposes families can mean just about any living arrangement (for example, foster care).

It is important to note that there are various definitions of a "child" for different purposes in the tax law. While there has been talk in Congress to adopt a single definition, no such rule has yet been adopted, so be sure to use the right definition of a child in each context.

This chapter covers the rules on dependency exemptions, tax benefits for adoption expenses, a number of different tax credits, and foster care payments. It also covers special relief for victims of terrorism and their families.

Personal and Dependency Exemptions

Each taxpayer can claim a personal exemption on his or her return. In addition, parents can claim a dependency exemption for each child or other dependent. There is no limit on the number of exemptions that can be claimed. The amount of each exemption for 2002 is $3,000 (up from $2,900 in 2001). Thus, a family of four—two parents and two children—will be able to deduct $400 more in 2002 compared with 2001 ($3,000 × 4 versus $2,900 × 4).

Caution

The higher exemption amount can be a detriment in certain cases. While it certainly boosts write-offs for regular tax purposes, those with a large number of dependents may find themselves subject to the alternative minimum tax. The reason: The personal and dependency exemptions are not deductible for AMT purposes (see Chapter 1). Thus, even middle-income taxpayers with large families may become liable for AMT.

PHASEOUT FOR HIGH EARNERS. If your adjusted gross income (AGI) exceeds a threshold amount, you lose some or all of the benefit of claiming personal exemptions. However, in

2002, due to cost-of-living adjustments, the phaseout starts at a higher income level than it did in 2001. The Table 2.1 compares the phaseout ranges for 2001 with those for 2002 based on your filing status. (Also see Examples 1 and 2.)

TABLE 2.1 Phaseout Ranges for Personal Exemptions

Filing Status	2001		2002	
	Beginning of Phaseout	End of Phaseout	Beginning of Phaseout	End of Phaseout
Married filing jointly	$199,450	$321,950	$206,000	$328,500
Head of household	166,200	288,700	171,650	294,150
Single	132,950	255,450	137,300	259,800
Married filing separately	99,725	160,975	103,000	164,250

Example 1

In 2002, the Browns, a married couple filing jointly, claim their two children as dependents. Their AGI is $150,000. Their deduction for exemptions is $12,000 ($3,000 × 4). There is no phaseout because their AGI is below $206,000.

Example 2

Same facts as in Example 1 except the couple's AGI is $350,000. Here they cannot deduct anything for their exemptions. Their AGI exceeds the phaseout limit of $328,500.

DEFINITION OF "CHILD." Any child of yours may qualify as a dependent as long as you provide more than half of his or her support and the child's gross income in 2002 does not exceed $3,000 (and certain other tests are met). If your child is under age 19 or is a full-time student under age 24, there is *no* gross income requirement. In other words, your child can earn any amount without your losing a dependency exemption as long as you provide more than half of the child's support.

Important: If you claim your child as a dependent he or she cannot be viewed as liberated for purposes of financial aid for college or graduate school. This means that your income and resources and your child's are considered in determining eligibility for financial aid. If your child is planning to attend graduate school, you may wish to forgo the dependency exemption in senior year so your student may apply for aid for graduate school based on his or her own income and resources.

SPECIAL RULE FOR A MISSING OR KIDNAPPED CHILD. A dependency exemption may be claimed for a missing or kidnapped child until the year in which the child is found or turns age 18 (whichever is earlier). The new law clarifies that a taxpayer who meets the principal place of abode test for determining whether a child is a dependent immediately before the kidnapping will continue to be treated as meeting the test until the terminating event (being found or turning 18). This, in turn, may enable a taxpayer to claim head of household or surviving spouse status. *Refund opportunity:* This clarification applies to tax years after

2000, so anyone who failed to claim head of household or surviving spouse status because of the principal place of abode test may want to claim a refund by filing an amended return.

LOOKING AHEAD

The phaseout of exemptions for high earners is set to be eliminated by 2010. This elimination is made in steps over five years but doesn't start until 2006.

Adoption Expenses

CREDIT AND EXCLUSION AMOUNT INCREASED. The tax law rewards by means of a tax credit parents who adopt a child if they pay expenses out of pocket. Alternatively, they may be eligible for an exclusion from income if an employer pays such expenses for them. These tax breaks are designed to offset to some degree the high cost of adoption, which ranges up to $2,500 for public agency adoptions to $30,000 or more for private agency fees.

The amount of the adoption credit has been increased in 2002 to $10,000 (up from $5,000, or $6,000 for a special needs child, in 2001). Similarly, the amount you can exclude for employer-paid expenses under a company's adoption assistance plan in 2002 is $10,000 (up from $5,000 in 2001).

LOOKING AHEAD

Starting in 2003, the $10,000 credit and the exclusion can be claimed for adoption of a special needs child without regard to actual expenses— the benefit is claimed simply for making the adoption.

INCOME LIMIT INCREASED.   The full credit and exclusion may be claimed only by taxpayers with modified AGI up to $150,000 in 2002 (up from $75,000 in 2001). The credit phases out so that no credit can be claimed once modified AGI exceeds $190,000 (up from $115,000 in 2001). *Important:* The same modified AGI limit applies regardless of filing status (that is, married couples filing jointly have the same limit as single parents). Married couples must file jointly to claim the credit or exclusion unless they live apart during the last six months of the year and file separate returns.

DEFINITION OF "CHILD."   A child for purposes of the adoption credit and exclusion is either anyone under the age of 18 or someone who is physically or mentally incapable of self-care regardless of age.

WHEN TO CLAIM THE CREDIT.   The timing of when you can claim the credit can be tricky. Timing depends on the nature of the child and when the adoption becomes final.

- *Non-special needs child who is a U.S. citizen or resident.* If the adoption is not final by the end of the year, then the credit can be claimed only in the year after the year in which payments have been made (even if the adoption is still not final). Expenses paid in the year in which the adoption is final are eligible for the credit at that time. Similarly, expenses paid in a later year (after the adoption is final) qualify for the credit at that later date. (See Example 3.)

- *Special needs child.* The credit may be claimed *only* in the year in which the adoption is final. (Prior to 2002,

Example 3

In 2002, Mr. and Mrs. Green pay $3,000 in adoption fees and expenses to adopt a child who is a U.S. citizen with no special needs. They pay an additional $8,000 in 2003. The adoption does not become final until February 1, 2004. No credit may be claimed on the Greens' 2002 return. However, the $3,000 paid in 2002 can be taken into account in figuring their credit for 2003. The Greens can use $7,000 of the fees paid in 2003 in figuring their credit for 2004. The remaining $1,000 cannot be used because they have reached the $10,000 limit.

the credit could have been claimed in the year following the year of payment even if the adoption was not yet final.) No credit may be claimed for expenses paid after the year the adoption becomes final.

- *Foreign child.* The credit may not be claimed until the year the adoption becomes final. Expenses paid in a later year qualify for the credit at that later time. (See Example 4.)

Example 4

In 2002, Mr. and Mrs. Grey pay $6,000 in adoption fees and expenses to adopt a child born and living abroad. They pay an additional $3,000 in 2003. The adoption does not become final until February 1, 2004. No credit may be claimed in 2002 or 2003. In 2004, the Greys may base their credit on $9,000 in adoption expenses.

LOOKING AHEAD

The $10,000 adoption credit limit and the $150,000 AGI phaseout limit may be adjusted for inflation.

Earned Income Credit

Low-income taxpayers may be eligible for a credit that encourages them to work. The credit is refundable—it can be paid to the taxpayer even if it exceeds the amount of tax for the year. In effect, it is a negative income tax designed to put money back into the pockets of low earners. However, this credit is highly complicated and produces more errors on tax returns that just about any other provision in the law. For example, some taxpayers assume they must support a child in order to claim the credit; but in reality the credit is available to low earners who have no qualifying child. Changes in the rules for the earned income credit do *not* make things any easier.

INCOME LIMITS INCREASED. For 2002, the definition of low earners is changed through cost-of-living adjustments that are made to certain limits. Table 2.2 shows the limits for 2002 based on the following definitions:

- "Earned income amount" is the amount of earned income at or above which the maximum credit can be claimed. For 2002, unlike in the past, earned income does not include any nontaxable benefits (for example, elective deferral contributions to 401(k) plans and employer-paid educational assistance). Effectively, earned income is the amount reported as wages on an employee's W-2 form or, for self-employed indi-

TABLE 2.2 Earned Income Credit Limits

Item	Number of Qualifying Children		
	One	Two or More	None
Earned income amount	$ 7,370	$10,350	$ 4,910
Maximum amount of credit	2,506	4,140	376
Threshold phaseout amount	13,520	13,520	6,150
Completed threshold amount	29,201	33,178	11,060
Threshold phaseout amount, married filing jointly	14,520	14,520	7,150
Completed phaseout amount, married filing jointly	30,201	34,178	12,060

viduals, the amount reported as net earnings from self-employment.

- "Threshold phaseout amount" is the greater of AGI or earned income above which the maximum credit starts to phase out.

- "Completed phaseout amount" is the greater of AGI or earned income at which no credit can be claimed.

UNEARNED INCOME LIMIT INCREASED. The credit cannot be claimed if unearned income—from interest, dividends, and other investments—exceeds a threshold amount. For 2002, the unearned income limit is $2,550 (up from $2,450 in 2001).

DEFINITION OF "CHILD." The relationships that can qualify a child have been broadened to include descendants of a stepchild. Thus, a qualifying child includes a child, stepchild, sibling, stepsibling, or descendant of any of these children.

A qualifying child must live with the taxpayer for at least six months. Before 2002, foster children were subject to a special one-year residency requirement; this has been eliminated so that foster children can be qualifying children if they, too, live with the taxpayer for over half of the taxable year.

OTHER CHANGES. The law now has a new test for determining which taxpayer can claim the credit when more than one individual meets eligibility requirements. As always, only one taxpayer can claim the credit with respect to a qualifying child. In the past, the tiebreaker used to determine which taxpayer could claim the credit was based on the higher adjusted gross income. Now, however, the child's parent has priority on claiming the credit. If both parents qualify, then priority goes to the parent with whom the child lived for the greater part of the year. If the child resided equally with each parent, then AGI is used to assign eligibility for the credit. Similarly, if neither eligible taxpayer is the child's parent, then AGI is used to assign eligibility for the credit as in the past.

In 2002, the earned income credit is not reduced by alternative minimum tax. Thus, even a taxpayer who is subject to the AMT can still claim the earned income credit (and use it to offset the AMT).

MARRIAGE PENALTY RELIEF AND THE EARNED INCOME CREDIT. See later in this chapter.

Child and Dependent Care Tax Credit

This credit is designed to assist taxpayers who incur care expenses in order to work. There is no change in the rules for the child and dependent care tax credit for 2002. But for planning purposes, keep in mind that there are important changes starting in 2003. The credit is set to increase substantially at that time. Here are some of the ways in which this credit will be expanded:

- The limit on expenses that can be taken into account in figuring the credit will increase to $3,000 for one eligible dependent and $6,000 for two or more eligible dependents (up from $2,400 and $4,800 respectively).

- The maximum percentage for figuring the credit is raised to 35 percent (up from 30 percent).

- The reduction in the credit starts at a higher income level—$15,000 (instead of $10,000). As a result, the minimum credit of 20 percent of eligible expenses starts at $43,000 (up from $28,000).

DEFINITION OF "CHILD." For purposes of this credit a child is an individual under age 13. A dependent can also be a spouse or other person of any age who is physically or mentally incapable of self-care (although a nonrelative must be a member of your household for the entire year).

Child Tax Credit

The tax law provides taxpayers with a credit simply for having a child. The credit amount for 2002 through 2004 is $600 per eligible child who is your dependent (the same as it was in 2001). At least a portion of the credit may be refundable—paid to you in excess of your tax liability. In 2002, the refundable amount is 10 percent of earned income from wages or self-employment in excess of $10,350 (up from $10,000 in 2001), up to the per child credit amount. (See Example 5.)

Taxpayers with three or more eligible children may figure their refundable credit under the pre-2001 rule (based on FICA or self-employment tax in excess of the earned income credit) if this produces a larger refund than under the 10 percent rule. (See Example 6.)

DEFINITION OF "CHILD." For purposes of this credit a child is any dependent under the age of 17 by the end of the year.

Example 5

In 2002, you have one qualifying child and earned income of $28,000. The refundable credit is $600 since this is less than $1,765 (10 percent of $28,000 – $10,350).

Example 6

In 2002, you have three qualifying children and your earned income is $28,000. You pay FICA of $2,142. Your earned income credit is $1,091. Under the 10 percent rule your refundable credit is $1,765 (10 percent of $28,000 – $10,350), which is less than your credit amount of $1,800 (3 children × $600). Under the old rule, your refundable portion would be $1,051. Thus, you rely on the 10 percent rule.

Marriage Penalty Relief

Under the current tax system, married couples can pay more tax than they would pay if they were single. This extra tax cost is referred to as a "marriage penalty" and generally affects all married couples whose incomes are split more evenly than 70/30. In future there will be a couple of law changes—changing the 15 percent tax bracket and standard deduction amounts for joint filers to twice the amount for singles—which are designed to reduce the marriage penalty. These changes, explained shortly, don't apply in 2002.

Marriage penalty relief is, however, available this year for certain provisions in the tax law. The marriage penalty is eased by increasing income limits on those who file joint returns. In effect, married persons filing jointly have double the income limits for singles.

HIGHER INCOME LIMITS FOR STUDENT LOAN INTEREST DEDUCTION. The income limit for deducting student loan interest from gross income for taxpayers who are married filing jointly has been doubled to the limit for singles. Those with AGI below the phaseout start can claim a full deduction of up to $2,500 in student interest paid in 2002. The limits are outlined in Table 2.3.

HIGHER INCOME LIMITS FOR CONTRIBUTORS TO COVERDELL EDUCATION SAVINGS ACCOUNTS (ESAs). The income limit for contributors who are married filing jointly has been doubled to the limit for singles. Those with AGI below the phaseout start can make a full contribution of up to $2,000 in 2002. The limits are outlined in Table 2.4.

Coverdell ESAs are explained in greater detail in Chapter 3.

TABLE 2.3 Phaseout Ranges for Student Loan Interest Deduction

Filing Status	Phaseout Start	Phaseout Completed
Married filing jointly	$100,000	$130,000
Other filing status	50,000	65,000

TABLE 2.4 Phaseout Ranges for Coverdell Education Savings Accounts

Filing Status	Phaseout Start	Phaseout Completed
Married filing jointly	$190,000	$220,000
Other filing status	95,000	110,000

HIGHER INCOME LIMITS FOR EARNED INCOME CREDIT. The phaseout limits for the earned income credit are adjusted slightly for married couples filing joint returns. For 2002, each phaseout range is increased by $1,000 for these taxpayers. (See Example 7.)

Other changes to the earned income credit were discussed earlier in this chapter.

STANDARD DEDUCTION. Starting in 2005, the standard deduction for joint filers starts to be increased so that by 2009 it will be double the amount allowed for singles. The tax standard deduction amount for joint filers will be the standard deduction amount for singles multiplied by the following percentage:

Tax Year	Applicable Percentage
2005	174%
2006	184
2007	187
2008	190
2009 and thereafter	200

Example 7

In 2002, a single taxpayer with one qualifying child has a phaseout range starting at $13,520. For a married couple with one qualifying child, the phaseout range starts at $14,520.

FIFTEEN PERCENT INCOME TAX BRACKET. The size of the 15 percent tax bracket will be increased for joint filers until it is double that for singles. However, this relief does not start to be phased in until 2005 and is not fully effective until 2008. The tax bracket for joint filers will be the bracket amount for singles multiplied by the following percentage:

Tax Year	Applicable Percentage
2005	180%
2006	187
2007	193
2008 and thereafter	200

Caution

At the time this book went to press Congress was considering acceleration of marriage penalty relief for the 15 percent income tax bracket. Under pending legislation, the relief would phase in starting in 2003 rather than in 2005.

Victims of Terrorism and Their Families

Those affected by the Oklahoma bombing of April 19, 1995; the terrorist attacks on September 11, 2001; or anthrax incidents after September 10, 2001, and before January 1, 2002, may be eligible for a variety of special tax relief.

WAIVER OF INCOME TAX. The estates of those who died in one of these incidents are relieved of *any* federal income tax liability for the year of death and the preceding year. The law provides a minimum tax benefit of $10,000, which can be claimed if total liability for the year of death and the preceding year is less than $10,000. (See Example 8.)

Refund opportunity: To obtain this benefit, amended returns must be filed; the IRS will not automatically send out checks to eligible individuals or their estates.

EXCLUSION OF DEATH BENEFITS. Families who receive death benefits paid by an employer on account of an incident may exclude the benefits from income. There is no dollar limit on this exclusion.

PAYMENTS FROM CHARITABLE ORGANIZATIONS. Terrorist victims and their families who receive payments from one of the many charitable organizations in existence or set up to specially provide assistance for needs arising from terrorist

---

Example 8

Jane was killed in the World Trade Center attack on September 11, 2001. Her tax liability for 2000 was $4,000. Her tax liability for 2001 was $5,000. She owes no federal income tax for 2000 and 2001, and her estate may recover any tax paid in 2000 and 2001. In addition, her estate will receive a payment of $1,000 ($10,000 – [$4,000 + $5,000]).

attacks can exclude the payments from income. Again, there is no dollar limit on this exclusion.

FORGIVENESS OF DEBT. Generally, when a creditor forgives repayment of any portion of a debt and the debtor is solvent, that forgiveness is treated as income. However, there is no income resulting from forgiveness arising out of the terrorist events.

DISASTER RELIEF PAYMENTS. Payments to cover personal, family, living, or funeral costs can be excluded from income. (This includes payments from airlines made to victims' families.) Similarly payments to cover the repair of a personal residence and the replacement of its contents can be excluded from income.

For more information about special tax relief for victims of terrorism, see IRS Publication 3920, "Tax Relief for Victims of Terrorist Attacks," at www.irs.gov.

Foster Care Payments

Foster care payments are not taxable to the recipient. These are payments made by a qualified foster care placement agency. The new law liberalizes the definition of a qualified foster care placement agency to include *any* such agency and not merely a state agency.

DEFINITION OF "CHILD." Foster care payments must be made on account of the placement of a qualified foster care individual in a home. This now includes *any* individual placed by a qualified foster care placement agency. In the past, it was limited to children no more than 18 years old. Thus, placement today of physically or mentally handicapped individuals may entitle foster caregivers to exclude payments from their income.

CHAPTER 3

Tax Relief for Educational Expenses

The cost of higher education continues to escalate faster than the ordinary rate of inflation. According to the College Board, over a 10-year period ending in 2001, after adjusting for inflation, the cost of tuition and fees at public institutions rose by 40 percent and at private institutions by 33 percent. The average annual cost at a four-year public institution for tuition, fees, room, and board last year was $10,136; at a private college $24,340; and at an Ivy League school $34,473. In order to help meet the challenge of paying these costs Congress has created various incentives. The tax law encourages you to save for higher education and helps you pay for education costs for yourself and your family by means of exclusions, deductions, and tax credits. There have been many favorable changes in this area of the tax law to provide you with greater tax savings than ever before.

In this chapter, you will learn about education-related exclusions—for interest on U.S. savings bonds, employer-provided education assistance, and scholarships and fellowships. You will also learn about deductions you can take for student loan interest, higher education costs, and teachers' out-of-pocket expenses. You'll find out about new rules for education savings plans—qualified tuition programs (529 plans) and Coverdell education savings accounts (ESAs). Finally, you'll learn about tax credits you can claim for higher education—the Hope credit and the lifetime learning credit.

Interest on Savings Bonds

You can exclude from income the interest earned on U.S. savings bonds—series EE or I—that you redeem to pay for qualified higher education costs for yourself, your spouse, or a dependent. The exclusion applies only to interest on bonds purchased in your name after 1989 (and you were at least 24 years old at the time of purchase).

You can claim the exclusion only if your modified adjusted gross income (MAGI) is no more than a set limit. This limit is adjusted annually for inflation. Table 3.1 shows the 2002 MAGI limit for fully or partially excluding savings bond interest based on your filing status. (Also see Example 1.)

TABLE 3.1 Savings Bond Interest Exclusion

Filing Status	Full Exclusion for MAGI Up To—	Exclusion Phaseout Range
Single (including head of household)	$57,600	$57,600 to $72,600
Married filing jointly	$86,400	$86,400 to $116,400

Example 1

You're single and redeem bonds in 2002 to pay for your child's college tuition. Interest on the redeemed bonds is $4,000 (all of which is used to pay qualified costs). If your MAGI is $65,100, you may exclude $2,000 of interest from your income.

Employer-Paid Education Assistance

You may exclude up to $5,250 of employer-paid education assistance provided to you under a company's plan. Starting in 2002, this exclusion applies to graduate as well as undergraduate courses.

Important: There is no dollar limit on the exclusion for employer-paid education assistance for any job-related courses. This is fully excluded as a working condition fringe benefit (an expense that would be deductible by you if you had paid for it). For example, if you work in data processing and your employer pays $6,000 for you to take a course on the latest computer system, you aren't taxed on any portion of this payment—it's fully excludable as a working condition fringe benefit (since you could have fully deducted this job-related education expense if you had paid for it).

Scholarships and Fellowships

Scholarships and fellowships to degree candidates continue to be tax free. This exclusion applies only to the portion of grants covering tuition, fees, books, and supplies. It does not apply to amounts for room and board, incidental expenses, or payments for services required as a condition of receiving the grants.

In the past, recipients of scholarships from the National Health Service Corps (NHSC) Scholarship Program or the Armed Forces Scholarship Program for tuition, fees, books, supplies, and equipment were taxed on these benefits because of their promise to render future services. As a result they paid on average about 37 percent of the monthly stipend in federal income tax withholding.

Starting in 2002, scholarships paid to degree candidates from these programs are treated the same as those paid to other degree candidates. As such, awards are excluded from gross income. This is so even though there is a future service obligation in connection with these particular scholarships.

As in the case of all scholarships and fellowships, the exclusion for scholarships from NHSC and the Armed Forces Scholarship Program does not apply to amounts paid for living expenses (such as room and board).

Student Loan Interest Deduction

Interest on student loans is deductible up to $2,500. This deduction is an adjustment to gross income; it is an "above-the-line" deduction that can be claimed regardless of whether other deductions are itemized.

For 2002, the interest is deductible as long as the loan is being repaid—the old 60-month limit that had allowed interest deductions only in the first 60 months of loan repayment has been removed. This means that those who have been paying off old loans and who were ineligible to claim a deduction in 2001 because of the 60-month limit may now be able to resume claiming student loan interest deductions. And those who take out additional loans for graduate school may be eligible for a deduction even though loans are paid off over periods exceeding 60 months. However, you cannot go back to any year before 2002 to deduct interest because of the elimination of the 60-month rule. (See Example 2.)

Example 2

You graduated from college in 1995 and have been paying off your student loans ever since January 1996. Because of the 60-month rule, you were unable to deduct any interest in 2001 (the 60-month period ended in 2000). In 2002, you can again deduct interest paid during the year (if your income is within set limits). But you can't amend your 2001 return to deduct any interest paid in that year—it precedes 2002.

LOOKING AHEAD

The MAGI limits for student loan interest deductions will be indexed for inflation starting in 2003.

The deduction can be claimed only if your modified adjusted gross income (MAGI) is below set amounts. For 2002, the MAGI limit has been increased for both singles and married couples. Table 3.2 shows the point at which the deduction starts to phase out and the point at which MAGI is too high to allow any deduction to be claimed.

Deduction for Education Costs

Tuition and Fees Deduction

An entirely new tax deduction may be claimed for those who pay higher education costs in 2002. Like the student interest deduction, the deduction for higher education costs is an adjustment to gross income (an above-the-line deduction) that can be claimed regardless of whether other deductions are itemized.

The maximum deduction is $3,000 per year of eligible

TABLE 3.2 Student Loan Interest Deduction Phaseout Ranges

Filing Status	Full Deduction if MAGI is Below—	No Deduction If MAGI Is Above—
Single (including head of household)	$ 50,000	$ 65,000
Married filing jointly	$100,000	$130,000

higher education expenses—tuition and fees. However, the maximum deduction may be claimed only by taxpayers with MAGI below a set limit. *Important:* There is no phaseout of the deduction—even $1 of excess MAGI prevents you from claiming the deduction. Those in danger of losing out on this deduction because of potentially excess MAGI should review the strategies in Chapter 1 on keeping AGI down.

The deduction for higher education costs is set to increase in 2004 and expires at the end of 2005. Table 3.3 shows the maximum deduction for qualified expenses.

TABLE 3.3 Maximum Deductions for Qualified Higher Education Expenses

Year	MAGI	Maximum Deduction
2002 and 2003	$65,000 or less if single* $130,000 or less if married filing jointly	$3,000
	More than $65,000 if single* More than $130,000 if married filing jointly	None
2004 and 2005	$65,000 or less if single* $130,000 or less if married filing jointly	$4,000
	More than $65,000 but not more than $80,000 if single* More than $130,000 but not more than $160,000 if married filing jointly	$2,000
	More than $80,000 if single* More than $160,000 if married filing jointly	None

*Single includes head of household.

Itemized Deduction for Education Costs

If you pay for job-related education costs and you can't deduct them as an above-the-line tuition and fees deduction (because, for instance, your income is over the limit), you may still be able to enjoy a tax write-off for these expenses. These costs continue to be deductible as a miscellaneous itemized deduction subject to the 2 percent floor if the courses are taken to maintain or improve your job skills or are required by your employer as a condition of employment, and the courses don't qualify you for a new trade or business.

Note: This deduction is quite broad and includes more items than the tuition and fees deduction. For example, this deduction includes travel costs to and from classes and books and supplies. Thus, if eligible, you can claim an above-the-line deduction for tuition and fees and an itemized deduction for expenses (such as travel and books) that do not qualify for the above-the-line deduction.

Educators' Out-of-Pocket Expenses

According to a 1996 study by the National Education Association, grade school teachers paid on average $400 each year on classroom supplies for which they did not receive any reimbursement. The law now gives them a modest tax break.

Educators who pay for classroom supplies out of their own pockets can now, for the first time, claim an above-the-line deduction for these expenses—up to $250 per year for

2002 and 2003. If you qualify, the deduction can be claimed even if you do not itemize other deductions.

The term "educators" includes not only teachers but also counselors, principals, and aides working at least 900 hours during the school year in grades K through 12. "Supplies" means ordinary and necessary expenses, including books, computer equipment, software, and supplementary materials, as well as athletic supplies for courses of instruction in health or physical education. Keep receipts to substantiate your expenditures.

Caution

The exclusion for an educator's out-of-pocket expenses is limited to amounts in excess of certain other exclusions (savings bond interest, distributions from 529 plans, and distributions from Coverdell ESAs).

529 Plans

You may be able to save for your child's or grandchild's college education through a tax-advantaged qualified tuition plan—referred to as a 529 plan after the section of the Internal Revenue Code that governs it. There are two types of 529 plans:

- *Prepaid tuition plans.* Contributions are applied toward guaranteed tuition payments (even if tuition costs increase).

- *Savings-type plans.* Contributions are invested by plan managers, and funds available for college costs depend on the plan's investment performance.

Previously only states could set up 529 plans. Starting in 2002, private institutions are permitted to set up pre-paid tuition plans (but not savings-type plans). Thus, for example, parent's who know their child will attend a certain Ivy League school on a legacy admission may wish to contribute to the school's 529 plan (if one has been set up). Private institutions must receive Internal Revenue Service (IRS) approval for their plans before accepting contributions.

OVERVIEW. While contributions to 529 plans are *not* deductible for federal income tax purposes, there are significant tax benefits to these savings arrangements:

- Income earned within the plan is tax deferred (and may become tax free).
- Distributions withdrawn from the plan for qualified higher education costs can be tax free.
- Amounts not used by one beneficiary can be used by another family member simply by the contributor(s) designating a new beneficiary.
- Contributions may be deductible for state income tax purposes. For example, New York allows each taxpayer an annual contribution deduction of $5,000 (or

$10,000 by a married couple) regardless of the number of beneficiaries for whom contributions are made.

- Contributions can be used for estate planning reasons even though contributors retain control over the plan. This is discussed later in this chapter.

PLAN DISTRIBUTIONS. Distributions from state 529 plans to beneficiaries for the payment of qualified education costs are now tax free. Prior to 2002, such amounts were taxable to the beneficiary at the beneficiary's tax rate. Starting in 2004, distributions or disbursements from private institutions also qualify for tax-free treatment.

Distributions that are not used for qualified education purposes (for example, distributions that are taken to pay for the beneficiary's wedding) are taxable. In addition they are subject to a 10 percent penalty (before 2002 each plan was required to impose its own *de minimis* penalty, which generally ranged from 10 percent to 15 percent). The 10 percent penalty does not apply in certain cases:

- Death or disability of the beneficiary.
- Receipt of a scholarship.

PLAN INVESTMENTS.   Generally contributors may not have any control over investments made in the plan. Plan managers (such as Fidelity and TIAA-CREF) decide on investments, including asset allocations, on the basis of the beneficiary's age and other factors. However, as a practical matter, you do retain a measure of control over investments:

- You may be able to select from a menu of investment options.
- You can switch investment choices. The IRS now allows such changes to be made once a year and whenever the beneficiary designation changes.
- You can roll over plan assets from one state plan to another one that offers the types of investments you prefer. *Note:* There may be plan-imposed restrictions on plan withdrawals.

ESTATE PLANNING.   You may remove substantial assets from your estate on a gift tax free basis by contributing to a 529 plan, apparently even though you effectively retain control over the account. The beneficiary need not be your child or even your grandchild—you may wish to fund a plan for a niece, nephew, or other relative.

In 2002, you can contribute up to $55,000 gift tax free. A special rule allows you to treat your contribution as being made equally over five years and to apply your annual gift tax exclusion to each year. Since the annual gift tax exclusion in 2002 is $11,000 (up from $10,000 in 2001), $55,000 is effectively shielded by this exclusion over the five-year period. (See Example 3.)

If your spouse joins in making the contribution, together you can contribute up to $110,000 gift tax free per beneficiary.

Note: If you die before the end of the five-year period, any excludable amount remaining is included in your gross estate. (See Example 4.)

Example 3

In 2002, you want to make sizable contributions to 529 plans on behalf of your five grandchildren so they'll have the funds for college and you'll reduce the size of your estate. You can contribute up to $275,000 in 2002 without any gift tax, but you do have to file a gift tax return to elect this special treatment. Assuming when you die your estate is in the 45 percent tax bracket, the contribution saves your family $123,750 in estate taxes.

Example 4

Same facts as in Example 3 except that you die in 2004, before the end of the five-year gift period. Here you've used up your exclusion in 2002, 2003, and 2004, but not in 2005 and 2006. Thus, two-fifths of the gift ($275,000 × $2/_5$), or $110,000, is included in your estate.

Caution

Estate tax and generation-skipping transfer tax implications of 529 plans are not entirely clear. Final regulations on the estate and generation-skipping ramifications have not yet been issued. It is important to discuss any substantial funding of these plans with your tax adviser.

OTHER TAX CHANGES FOR 2002. Law changes have made a number of favorable revisions to 529 rules:

- You may contribute to both 529 plans and Coverdell ESAs (discussed in the next section) in the same year.
- Members of the family for whom rollovers of 529 accounts can be made now include first cousins of the original beneficiary. In the past members of the family included only siblings, grandchildren, aunts, and uncles.
- There is no fixed dollar limit for room and board distributions. In the past, there had been a $2,500 limit for nonschool housing ($1,500 for those living at home). Now the limit is the amount the school allocates for purposes of federal financial aid programs. However, as in the past, in order to treat distributions for room and board as qualified expenses the student must be enrolled at least part-time.

In deciding whether to contribute to a 529 plan and, if so, which plan to select, be sure to compare the contribution limits, plan managers, fees, and other aspects of state plans. For further information (including state-by-state comparisons), see the Appendix or visit www.saving forcollege.com.

Coverdell Education Savings Accounts

Coverdell education savings accounts (ESAs), formerly called education IRAs, are another tax-advantaged education savings-type vehicle. Like 529 plans, no federal income tax deduction is allowed for contributions. And, like 529 plans, distributions from Coverdell ESAs used for qualified education purposes are tax free.

Coverdell ESAs offer several unique advantages over 529 plans:

- Contributors can control investments while building up a savings fund for the beneficiary.
- Distributions can be used not only for higher education purposes, but also for elementary and secondary school—both public and private (before 2002 they were restricted to higher education costs). Thus, disbursements can now be made tax free for the payment of tuition to religious day schools.
- Qualified expenses include not only tuition and room and board, but in 2002 and later also related expenses—computer technology and equipment (e.g., a computer, software, peripherals, and Internet access; academic tutoring;

uniforms; transportation; and supplementary items and services (e.g., extended day programs).

- Contributions for the year may be made up to the due date of the tax return. For example, contributions for 2002 can be made up to April 15, 2003, and this contribution is treated as having been made on December 31, 2002.

However, there are considerable restrictions on Coverdell ESAs that don't apply to 529 plans. These restrictions on Coverdell ESAs include:

- Annual contributions to Coverdell ESAs are limited to $2,000 per year per beneficiary (up from $500 per year in 2001). There is no federal tax law limit on contributions to 529 plans.
- A contributor's MAGI cannot exceed a set dollar amount as set forth in Table 3.4. These dollar limits reflect new amounts for 2002, which remove the marriage penalty. The MAGI limit applies only to contributors who are individuals (prior to 2002, the limit applied to all contributors, effectively barring

TABLE 3.4 Coverdell Education Savings Account Contributions

Filing Status	Full Contribution If MAGI Is No More Than—	Contribution Phaseout Range
Single (including head of household)	$ 95,000	$ 95,000 to $110,000
Married filing jointly	$190,000	$190,000 to $220,000

corporations from making contributions on behalf of employees' children). There is no MAGI limit on contributors to 529 plans.

- Contributions can be made only for someone who is under age 18, and distributions must be made (or are treated as having been made) at age 30. However, starting in 2002 these age restrictions do not apply to a special needs beneficiary. This is someone who, due to a physical, mental, or emotional impairment (including a learning disability) requires additional time to complete his or her education.

EXCESS DISTRIBUTIONS. When an education credit is claimed in the same year in which distributions are taken from an ESA, education expenses are first taken into account in figuring the credit. Where distributions exceed qualified expenses, the excess is included in gross income. (See Example 5.)

Example 5

You have contributed to a Coverdell ESA for your child who will attend college in the fall of 2002. To cover costs of $2,500, $2,500 is withdrawn from the ESA. You claim a Hope credit of $1,500 (based on $2,000 of education expenses). Education expenses are first taken into account for the education credit. Thus the excess ESA distribution of $500 ($2,500 qualified expenses reduced by $2,000, those used for the higher education credit) is subject to tax. For a full discussion of the education credit, see *J.K. Lasser's Your Income Tax, 2003*.

WAIVER OF THE 10 PERCENT PENALTY. Where distributions from ESAs are included in income solely because an education credit is claimed, the 10 percent penalty on ESA distributions does not apply. In effect, if the distributions from the ESA *would have been excluded* had no credit been claimed—the funds are used to pay qualified education costs—then the 10 percent penalty is waived. Thus, in Example 5, the $500 excess ESA distribution included in income because of claiming an education credit does not result in a 10 percent penalty.

EXCESS CONTRIBUTIONS. Suppose a beneficiary's parent and aunt each contribute $2,000 to a Coverdell ESA for the same year. The law allows excess contributions to be withdrawn penalty free. (If the overfunding remains in the account there is a 6 percent excess contribution penalty imposed each year.)

In the past, the deadline for withdrawing excess contributions penalty free was the due date of the beneficiary's return (including filing extensions) or April 15 of the year following the contribution year if the beneficiary isn't required to file a return. For 2002, the deadline has been extended to May 31 of the year following the year of the contribution. (See Example 6.)

Planning Strategies for Coverdell ESAs

Those prevented from making a contribution because of the MAGI limit can, of course, gift such funds to someone else

> ## Example 6
>
> In 2002, two separate taxpayers each contribute $1,500 to a Coverdell ESA for Junior. The excess contribution—$1,000—must be withdrawn (taken back by the contributor) no later than May 31, 2003. If there are two separate ESAs, excess amounts can be withdrawn from one or more of them as long as the total excess amount is withdrawn.

whose MAGI is within set limits, and then that person can make the contribution.

Those who own closely held corporations are in a unique position to have their children's education funded through company contributions. Since there is no MAGI limit on corporate contributors, your personal MAGI is irrelevant. However, corporate contributions on your behalf may constitute taxable dividends, so be sure to consult with a tax adviser before arranging any such contributions.

Individuals who do not expect their children or grandchildren to need financial aid may want to contribute to *both* Coverdell ESAs and qualified tuition plans in order to save as much as possible in tax-advantaged savings vehicles.

Education Tax Credits

If you pay for higher education costs for yourself, your spouse, or your dependent, you may be eligible to claim an education credit. (Remember that a tax credit is worth more than a deduction since it reduces your tax liability on a dollar-for-dollar basis.) You can claim the credit even if you borrow the money to pay the education costs. There are two types of education credits:

- *Hope credit.* The credit is 100 percent of qualified tuition and related fees up to $1,000 and 50 percent of such expenses in excess of $1,000, for a top credit of $1,500. The credit applies only to the first two years of a student's higher education. The credit is figured on a per student basis. Thus, if your twins are both freshmen in college, you can claim a total credit of up to $3,000.

- *Lifetime learning credit.* The credit is 20 percent of the first $5,000 in qualified tuition and related fees, for a top credit of $1,000. The credit can be claimed for any higher education and applies on a per taxpayer basis. Thus, if you claim the credit for expenses you paid for yourself and for your child who is a senior in college, your total credit is limited to $1,000.

INCOME LIMITS. The credit may be claimed only if your MAGI is below set limits. In 2002, the income limits have been increased for the first time, as shown in Table 3.5.

Important: If your MAGI prevents you from claiming the credit, your child may be able to do so—even though you paid the expenses. In order for your child to claim the credit, you must waive a dependency exemption for him or

TABLE 3.5 Income Limits for Higher Education Credits

Filing Status	Full Credit If MAGI Is No More Than—	Credit Phaseout Range
Single (including head of household)	$41,000	$41,000 to $51,000
Married filing jointly	$82,000	$82,000 to $102,000

her (an action that may not result in any tax increase to you if your exemptions are already phased out because of your high income). Also, your child must have tax liability (for example, resulting from mutual fund distributions) in order to benefit from the credit. In deciding whether to let your child claim the credit, weigh the tax savings you'd receive from claiming the exemption against the tax savings to your child, and choose the option that provides the greater tax benefit for the family.

COORDINATION OF EDUCATION CREDITS AND DISTRIBUTIONS FROM COVERDELL ESAs AND/OR 529 PLANS. In figuring whether credits can be claimed in the same year in which distributions are taken from Coverdell ESAs, expenses are taken into account first for the education credits. If distributions are taken from both Coverdell ESAs and qualified tuition plans, then expenses

LOOKING AHEAD

Starting in 2003, the lifetime learning credit increases to 20 percent of $10,000 of qualified education expenses. Also, the income limits may again be adjusted for inflation. Further, the amount of expenses taken into account in figuring the Hope credit may be increased for inflation.

must be allocated between them if total distributions exceed total reduced expenses (expenses after they have been taken into account for an education credit).

The law does not set forth any particular method for making such an allocation. However, it seems reasonable to make an allocation based on a ratio of the distribution from the Coverdell ESA and 529 plan to total distributions from both. (See Example 7.)

Example 7

In 2002, when qualified higher education costs are $14,000, $10,000 is distributed from a 529 plan and $2,000 from a Coverdell ESA to pay for your child's higher education costs. Qualified expenses are first reduced by $5,000 taken into account in figuring a lifetime learning credit for your child (who is a junior in college). An allocation must be made of distributions from the Coverdell ESA and 529 plan in order to determine whether and how much of each distribution is taxable. The reduced expenses of $9,000 ($14,000 – $5,000) are allocated as follows:

529 plan: $7,500 ($9,000 × [$10,000 ÷ $12,000] = $7,500)
Coverdell ESA: $1,500 ($9,000 × [$2,000 ÷ $12,000] = $1,500)

Estate, Gift, and Generation-Skipping Transfer Tax Relief

Income taxes may not be your only tax concern. If you give away money during your lifetime or at your death, issued involving estate tax, gift tax and/or generation-skipping transfer tax (collectively referred to as transfer taxes) can arise. Is the money or property you give away or pass on subject to transfer taxes? Is it better to give your property away while you're alive or to wait until death (assuming you can afford to make this choice)? New rules allow you to transfer more of your assets to your family and friends—during lifetime or at death—without resulting in a transfer tax.

But the complexities of these transfer tax rules have grown immeasurably as a result of recent law changes. To add further complication, the future of these rules is uncertain. For example, the estate tax is set to be repealed in full in 2010, and then old estate tax rules (in effect in 2001) are set to reapply starting in 2011 unless Congress takes further action. While President Bush has been pushing for complete repeal and the House voted for it, budget considerations (and the need for revenue) may override his efforts.

The estate tax changes effective for 2002 are reflected in a revised Form 706, United States Estate (and Generation-Skipping Transfer Tax) Return. This revised form should be used for estates of decedents dying in 2002 and generation-skipping transfers made in 2002.

This chapter covers in detail the new rules for 2002 on estate, gift, and generation-skipping transfers. It also explains how limits on transfers will change in the coming years so you can devise long-range plans.

Estate Tax Changes

The old adage about the certainty of death and taxes applies doubly to estate taxes for those of means. Your estate generally can't escape paying a federal estate tax on the assets you own or have an interest in at death if their value exceeds a certain amount. (If you're married, you can arrange it so that the tax may be postponed until the death of whichever spouse dies second, but eventually some transfer tax will be paid.)

Exemption Amount

How rich do you have to be in order to be concerned about the federal estate tax? That figure increases in the coming years. For 2002 and 2003, there is no federal estate tax if your estate is valued at no more than $1 million (up from $675,000 in 2001). This exemption is accomplished by permitting your estate to claim a credit against the tax liability that effectively exempts $1 million from tax. Thus, in 2002 and 2003, the tax credit reflecting the $1 million exemption amount is $345,800.

LOOKING AHEAD

In 2004 and 2005, the estate tax exemption amount increases to $1.5 million. It increases to $2 million in 2006 and to $3.5 million in 2009. In 2010, there is no exemption amount—there is no need for one since there will be no estate tax in 2010. However, starting in 2011, unless Congress acts in the interim, the estate tax will be reinstated and the exemption will drop to $1 million and remain there.

PLANNING.   The increase in the exemption amount can affect you in one of two ways: Either you need no longer be concerned with federal estate tax because your assets are below the increased taxable threshold or you can pass on a greater amount without the imposition of federal estate tax.

But don't be too quick to dismiss the federal estate tax out of hand; the size of your estate may be larger than you think. Be sure to consider *all* your assets, including your IRAs and retirement benefits and inheritances you may come into. By making a thorough inventory of your assets (based on their present value), you'll get a better idea of whether you should be planning to reduce federal estate taxes or whether you're home free. Just remember that things can change. You may think you're currently exempt from worrying about the federal estate tax, but if you come into money (for example, an insurance settlement, lottery winnings, or an inheritance), you may then find yourself vulnerable to the federal estate tax. Or if the value of your assets rises (for example, the stock market recovers and boosts the value of your stocks and stock mutual funds held both personally and in retirement accounts), again you may find that the size of your estate is large enough to fall victim to estate tax—or at least the need to plan to minimize or avoid it.

Until now, a common estate planning strategy for married couples with sufficient assets to be subject to the federal estate tax was to set up a credit shelter or bypass trust so that the exemption amount could be fully used in the estate of the first spouse to die. It worked like this: A will provided that a credit shelter trust (also called a bypass trust) would be created with an amount equal to the maximum exemption amount. The surviving spouse would be named as the income beneficiary of that trust, enjoying income for life, with assets of the trust passing at the surviving spouse's death to other named beneficiaries (typically the couple's children). Assets in excess of the exemption amount placed in the trust would pass outright to the surviving spouse. Result: At the death of the first spouse there would be no estate tax. The assets passing directly to the surviving spouse would be shielded by the marital deduction, and the assets passing into the credit shelter trust would be shielded by the exemption amount. At the death of the surviving spouse, the assets in the trust are not included in that spouse's estate; they pass directly (untaxed) to the named beneficiaries.

If your existing will or a trust contains a formula clause for funding a credit shelter or bypass trust based on the "maximum federal exemption amount" or "maximum unified credit," you may wish to revise these documents. You may be passing on to that trust more than you intended, to the detriment of other heirs. For example, if your estate is worth $1.5 million and you die in 2002 with an old will providing for a credit shelter trust based on the maximum exemption amount, two-thirds of your estate will be in that trust, which may be more than you'd envisioned.

Discuss with your tax or legal adviser new ways to limit the amount of assets passing into a credit shelter or bypass trust. For example, you may wish to limit the funding of the trust to a set dollar amount or a percentage of the estate or some combination of these two limits.

Estate Tax Rates

Like federal income tax rates, estate tax rates are graduated—the larger your estate the higher the estate tax rate. In 2002, the top estate tax rate is 50 percent (down from 55 percent in 2001). In addition, the 5 percent surtax on very large estates that had applied in prior years is eliminated completely.

Table 4.1 shows the estate tax rates for an individual dying in 2002. The tentative tax is the tax *before* applying any

TABLE 4.1 Estate Tax Rates for Those Dying in 2002

Taxable Estate	Tentative Tax
Not over $10,000	18% of such amount
Over $10,000 but not over $20,000	$1,800, plus 20% of the amount over $10,000
Over $20,000 but not over $40,000	$3,800, plus 22% of the amount over $20,000
Over $40,000 but not over $60,000	$8,200, plus 24% of the amount over $40,000
Over $60,000 but not over $80,000	$13,000, plus 26% of the amount over $60,000
Over $80,000 but not over $100,000	$18,200, plus 28% of the amount over $80,000
Over $100,000 but not over $150,000	$23,800, plus 30% of the amount over $100,000
Over $150,000 but not over $250,000	$38,800, plus 32% of the amount over $150,000
Over $250,000 but not over $500,000	$70,800, plus 34% of the amount over $250,000
Over $500,000 but not over $750,000	$155,800, plus 37% of the amount over $500,000
Over $750,000 but not over $1,000,000	$248,300, plus 39% of the amount over $750,000
Over $1,000,000 but not over $1,250,000	$345,800, plus 41% of the amount over $1,000,000
Over $1,250,000 but not over $1,500,000	$448,300, plus 43% of the amount over $1,250,000
Over $1,500,000 but not over $2,000,000	$555,800, plus 45% of the amount over $1,500,000
Over $2,000,000 but not over $2,500,000	$780,800, plus 49% of the amount over $2,000,000
Over $2,500,000	$1,025,800, plus 50% of the amount over $2,500,000

tax credits, including the credit that reflects the exemption amount discussed earlier and the state death tax credit. These credits may effectively eliminate any estate tax liability. (See also Example 1.)

SPECIAL ESTATE TAX RATES FOR VICTIMS OF TERRORISM AND MILITARY PERSONNEL. More favorable tax rates can be used for estates of anyone dying as a result of the April 19, 1995, Oklahoma City attack; the September 11, 2001, terrorist attacks; or an anthrax incident occurring after September 10, 2001, and before January 1, 2002. They also apply to military personnel who die while serving in a combat zone after September 11, 2001.

The maximum estate tax rule under a special table incorporating favorable tax rates for these victims is 20 percent

LOOKING AHEAD

The top estate tax rate declines by one percentage point each year over the next several years (e.g., 49 percent in 2003), until it reaches 45 percent in 2007. It remains at 45 percent until 2010 when the estate tax is repealed entirely. However, starting in 2011, the former top estate tax rate of 55 percent will again apply (unless Congress acts in the interim).

Example 1

In 2002, Mrs. Smith dies with an estate valued at $2 million. (Assume there are no deductions.) The tentative tax on her estate is $780,800. Her estate tax liability is $435,000 ($780,800 minus tax credit amount of $345,800) (before application of the state death tax credit, if any).

(compared with 50 percent for other decedents). Table 4.2 shows the special tax rate schedule for estates of terrorist victims. The tentative tax is the amount before applying any credits, such as the credit for the exemption amount and the state death tax credit, which may eliminate any estate tax liability.

These favorable tax rates apply *unless* the executor elects not to have them apply. Unless the executor elects out, the designation "Section 2201" should be written at the top of the estate tax return, Form 706, and the special tax rates should be used. The estate of anyone filing under these special rates should send the estate tax return to the Internal Revenue Service, E&G Department/Stop 824T, 201 W. Rivercenter Blvd., Covington, KY 41011.

Refund opportunity: Estates of Oklahoma City victims may be entitled to a refund of the federal estate tax. To obtain a refund, an amended estate tax return must be filed. The statute of limitations for filing refund claims with respect to Oklahoma City victims is extended through January 22, 2003.

State Death Tax Credit

An estate may claim a tax credit for state death taxes paid by the estate. Until now, in 37 states and the District of Columbia the state estate tax amount has been equal to the federal state death tax credit. This state estate tax is referred to as a "pick-up tax" because it picks up the amount of the state death tax credit permitted to be claimed on the federal estate tax return.

TABLE 4.2 Estate Tax Rates for Terrorist Victims

Taxable Estate	Tentative Tax
Not over $100,000	None
Over $100,000 but not over $150,000	1% of such amount
Over $150,000 but not over $200,000	$500, plus 2% of the amount over $150,000
Over $200,000 but not over $300,000	$1,500, plus 3% of the amount over $200,000
Over $300,000 but not over $500,000	$4,500, plus 4% of the amount over $300,000
Over $500,000 but not over $700,000	$12,500, plus 5% of the amount over $500,000
Over $700,000 but not over $900,000	$22,500, plus 6% of the amount over $700,000
Over $900,000 but not over $1,100,000	$34,500, plus 7% of the amount over $900,000
Over $1,100,000 but not over $1,600,000	$48,500, plus 8% of the amount over $1,100,000
Over $1,600,000 but not over $2,100,000	$88,500, plus 9% of the amount over $1,600,000
Over $2,100,000 but not over $2,600,000	$133,500, plus 10% of the amount over $2,100,000
Over $2,600,000 but not over $3,100,000	$183,500, plus 11% of the amount over $2,600,000
Over $3,100,000 but not over $3,600,000	$238,500, plus 12% of the amount over $3,100,000
Over $3,600,000 but not over $4,100,000	$298,500, plus 13% of the amount over $3,600,000
Over $4,100,000 but not over $5,100,000	$363,500, plus 14% of the amount over $4,100,000

(Continued)

TABLE 4.2 *(Continued)*

Taxable Estate	Tentative Tax
Over $5,100,000 but not over $6,100,000	$503,500, plus 15% of the amount over $5,100,000
Over $6,100,000 but not over $7,100,000	$653,500, plus 16% of the amount over $6,100,000
Over $7,100,000 but not over $8,100,000	$813,500, plus 17% of the amount over $7,100,000
Over $8,100,000 but not over $9,100,000	$983,500, plus 18% of the amount over $8,100,000
Over $9,100,000 but not over $10,100,000	$1,163,500, plus 19% of the amount over $9,100,000
Over $10,100,000	$1,353,500, plus 20% of the amount over $10,100,000

LOOKING AHEAD

The state death tax credit is further reduced in 2003 (by 50 percent of the amount otherwise allowed) and in 2004 (by 75 percent of the amount otherwise allowed). No credit may be claimed after 2004. After 2004, the credit is replaced by a deduction for the actual amount of state death taxes paid by an estate. The value of the deduction is clearly worth less than a credit.

It is unclear how the state estate tax will be figured in those states starting in 2002. The reason: In 2002, the federal tax credit begins to be phased out, so that the state's share of taxes at death is effectively reduced. In several states, including Florida, Pennsylvania, New Hampshire, New Jersey, and New York, the pick-up tax accounts for more than 2 percent of total state revenues. Expect to see some states amend their estate tax laws or make up the revenue shortfall in other ways.

In 2002, the state death tax credit is reduced by 25 percent of the amount otherwise allowed. Thus, the maximum state death tax credit for an adjusted taxable estate over $10,040,000 is $812,100, plus 12 percent of the amount over $10,040,000.

The impact of the change in the state death tax credit may be a *higher* total tax burden on estates than before the reduction in federal estate taxes. The reason: Some states do not automatically adopt changes in federal estate tax law so that prior limits apply. (See Example 2.)

Miscellaneous Estate Tax Changes

There are a number of changes that can affect the computation of the federal estate tax. Some of these changes are

---

Example 2

In New York, the federal estate tax law in existence on July 22, 1998, continues to govern the state's death taxes. As a result, unless the state legislature takes action, the state's death tax will be an amount equal to a 16 percent federal state death tax credit (the 12 percent in existence for federal tax purposes, plus 4 percent additional state tax). Thus, the combined top federal and state estate tax is 54 percent (50 percent for federal estate tax and an additional 4 percent for New York estate tax).

---

minor or merely technical in nature, but others can have a significant impact on the amount of taxes that will be paid.

LOOKING AHEAD

The limit for special use valuation will continue to be adjusted annually for inflation (regardless of any changes in federal estate tax rates or exemption amounts).

SPECIAL USE VALUATION. If an estate includes a farm or property used in a business, it can be valued at its special use rather than at its highest and best use. However, the reduction in the size of the gross estate through special use valuation cannot exceed a set dollar amount. For 2002, the limit has increased to $820,000 (up from $800,000).

CONSERVATION EASEMENTS. A conservation easement is a right given to a charitable organization or a government body to use land for recreation, the preservation of open space, or plant or wildlife refuges. The executor of an estate may elect to exclude a percentage of land subject to a conservation easement or the exclusion limit, whichever is less. The percentage is 40 percent, reduced by 2 percentage points for each percentage point by which the value of the easement is less than 30 percent of the value of the property. The exclusion limit increased for 2002 and later years to $500,000 (up from $400,000 in 2001). (See Example 3.)

INTEREST ON THE PORTION OF THE ESTATE TAX PAYABLE IN INSTALL-MENTS. Certain estates can qualify to pay federal estate tax in installments over 14 years. This payout option is designed

Example 3

You specify that upon your death acreage behind your home shall be set aside as a conservation easement. The value of that acreage is $250,000 and the value of the easement is $50,000. This value is 10 percentage points below the 30 percent threshold, so the 40 percent exclusion amount is reduced by 20 percentage points (2 × 10 percentage points) to 20 percent. The exclusion is $10,000 ($50,000 × 20 percent, which is less than the top exclusion of $500,000).

to permit estates heavily comprised of business interests to avoid liquidating those interests to pay the taxes.

If the estate is eligible and elects this installment payment option, then a portion of the federal estate tax is subject to a favorable interest rate of only 2 percent. The dollar amount used to determine the 2 percent portion increased in 2002 to $1.1 million (up from $1,060,000 in 2001).

LOOKING AHEAD

Like the limit on special use valuation, the dollar limit on the portion of the estate tax payment in installments that qualifies for the favorable interest rate will continue to be indexed annually for inflation.

What's Not Changed in Estate Tax

It's important to recognize that certain basic rules of the federal estate tax remain unchanged by the new law. Fundamentals include the following:

- An unlimited marital deduction for property passing to a surviving spouse.
- An unlimited charitable contribution deduction for property passing to charity.
- A deduction for estate expenses, indebtedness, and certain taxes.
- A deduction for family-owned business interests of up to $675,000 for 2002 and 2003. This deduction is repealed starting in 2004. However, any recapture of the deduction for dispositions of the interests by the family within 10 years of death continues to apply.
- Alternate valuation date for valuing property included in the estate, which is generally six months after the date of death.
- Special use valuation for valuing farms and business realty.
- The credit for tax on prior transfers. However, starting in 2005, the computation of the credit is changed slightly.

Gift Tax Changes

A quarter of a century ago, the estate and gift taxes became unified—that is, subject to the same tax rates and the same exemption amounts. Now they have effectively been decoupled so that different rates and exemption amounts will apply in the coming years.

Lifetime Gift Tax Exemption Amount

You may give away in your lifetime a set amount without any gift tax. For 2002, the gift tax exemption amount, like the estate tax exemption amount, increases to $1 million (up from $675,000 in 2001). However, the gift tax exemption will not be further increased—it will not even be indexed for inflation. (The estate tax exemption amount increases to $1.5 million in 2004.)

PLANNING.   Those who used up their lifetime gift tax exemption amounts before 2002 can make additional tax-free gifts at this time. However, because the gift tax is figured on cumulative gifts, the additional tax-free amount is not simply $325,000 (the difference between the new $1 million exemption limit and the old $675,000 limit); it is less than about $303,000.

GIFTS TO NON-U.S. CITIZEN SPOUSES. While gifts to spouses who are U.S. citizens can be made in any amount—there are no percentage or dollar limits—a dollar limit is imposed on transfers to non-U.S. citizen

> **LOOKING AHEAD**
>
> The exemption limit on gifts to non-U.S. citizen spouses will continue to be indexed annually for inflation.

spouses (including spouses who are permanent U.S. residents). In 2002 the limit increases to $110,000 (up from $106,000 in 2001).

LOOKING AHEAD

The top federal gift tax rate, like the federal estate tax rate, declines by one percentage point each year over the next several years (e.g., 49 percent in 2003), until it reaches 45 percent in 2007. It remains at 45 percent through 2009. In the year in which the estate tax is repealed—2010—the gift tax remains (the gift tax isn't repealed along with the estate tax). At that time, the gift tax rates will be changed to marginal rates ranging from 18 percent to 35 percent. The top rate will apply to taxable gifts over $500,000. In effect, the top gift tax rate of 35 percent will be the same as the top individual income tax rate at that time.

Gift Tax Rates

For 2002, the gift tax rates are the same as the estate tax rates. Thus, the maximum gift tax rate is 50 percent (down from 55 percent in 2001).

Annual Gift Tax Exclusion

Without regard to your lifetime exemption amount, each year you can give away a set amount to as many people as you choose without any gift tax—without even having to file a gift tax return. This is called an annual gift tax exclusion.

In 2002, the annual exclusion has been adjusted for inflation to $11,000 (up from $10,000 in 2001). This means you can give away $11,000 to as many people as you wish. (See Example 4.)

Married couples can agree to make split gifts, thereby doubling the annual gift tax exclusion. In other words, together they can give any person $22,000 in 2002, even if the gifted money or property is owned by one spouse. How-

LOOKING AHEAD

The annual gift tax exclusion may be adjusted for inflation. Any adjustment will be in $1,000 increments.

Example 4

You have three children and five grandchildren. In 2002, you can give them each $11,000, or a total of $88,000, without any gift tax. Gifts offset by the annual gift tax exclusion do not use up any part of your lifetime exemption amount.

---

ever, if split gifts are made, a gift tax return must be filed even though no tax is due.

Generation-Skipping Transfer Tax Changes

Wealthy individuals whose children don't need an inheritance to improve their standard of living may give their money to their grandchildren. This strategy effectively saves estate tax on one generation (the children's generation), allowing grandchildren to inherit more property on an after-tax basis. Making a generation-skipping transfer—from grandparent to grandchild—may result in a special transfer tax, called the generation-skipping transfer (GST) tax. The GST tax is intended to collect the revenue lost by avoiding estate tax on the skipped generation. The GST tax is imposed in addition

LOOKING AHEAD

In 2003, the generation-skipping transfer exemption is again adjusted for inflation. Starting in 2004, however, the GST exemption becomes the same as the estate tax exemption (for example, $1.5 million in 2004 and 2005).

LOOKING AHEAD

As the top estate tax rate declines over the coming years as explained earlier, the GST tax rate is reduced accordingly. In 2010, when the federal estate tax is repealed, the GST tax similarly disappears. Then, in 2011, like the federal estate tax, the GST tax reappears—based on the law in effect in 2001. This means that the top GST rate again rises to 55 percent. The GST exemption amount will depend on inflation adjustments to the $1,060,000 limit for 2001.

to any other transfer tax (estate or gift tax). The rules on the GST tax for 2002 have changed.

GST Exemption Amount

The exemption amount that can be transferred across the generations without imposition of the GST tax has been adjusted for inflation to $1.1 million in 2002 (up from $1,060,000 in 2001). (See Example 5.)

Example 5

Grandma dies in 2002, leaving her $5 million estate as follows: $4 million to her only child and $1 million split equally among her three grandchildren. Her entire estate (less the exemption amount of $1 million) is subject to federal estate tax. There is no GST tax in this case because the GST to her grandchildren is less than her GST exemption amount of $1.1 million. Thus, if her son leaves the balance of his $4 million inheritance to his children at death, there's an estate tax savings on the $1 million (plus future appreciation) that has already passed from Grandma to her grandchildren. If the son dies after 2010 when the top estate tax rate returns to 55 percent, this could be a tax savings of as much as $550,000.

GST Tax Rate

The GST tax rate continues to be the highest federal estate tax rate. However, since the top estate tax rate declines in 2002 to 50 percent (from 55 percent in 2001), the GST rate is effectively reduced to 50 percent.

CHAPTER 5

Pension and IRA Relief

Retirement income generally comes from three sources: Social Security benefits, qualified retirement plans and IRAs, and personal savings. In order to have a financially secure retirement, you can't rely on Social Security benefits as your primary source. And today it's difficult to save money for retirement in personal accounts after paying your current bills (including taxes) and other expenses and saving for other purposes (such as the purchase of a home or a child's college education). So the main way for most people to provide a comfortable retirement income is through retirement plans and IRAs. Fortunately, recent law changes make it easier than ever to save more money on a tax-advantaged basis.

There are two tax aspects to retirement savings—putting money into tax-advantaged accounts and taking money out of these accounts. During your working years you're building up retirement savings through contributions to 401(k) plans and personal IRAs. At retirement you're tapping into these funds, balancing two key considerations: what you need to live on and what the law requires you to take in order to avoid penalties.

This chapter explains the new retirement savings opportunities—new contribution limits for 2002 and thereafter and new tax incentives to encourage you to save in retirement plans. This chapter also discusses the new, highly favorable rules on taking required distributions from qualified plans and IRAs so, if you are financially able to get by with other funds, you can withdraw as little as possible from these accounts without incurring any tax penalties.

Contribution Limits

Forget what you knew up to now about the dollar limits on contributions to retirement plans and IRAs. The rules have changed completely—for the better. New limits apply for 2002 and they'll continue to increase in the coming years. The new limits present you with an important opportunity to save for your retirement on a tax-advantaged basis. (See Example 1.)

There are two ways in which contributions are made—cash contributions and elective deferrals (designating under a salary reduction agreement to use part of your salary *before tax* as your plan contribution amount). Cash contri-

Example 1

If you're eligible to contribute to a deductible IRA in 2002 and make the maximum contribution for someone under age 50 ($3,000), the government effectively contributes up to $1,158 if you're in the top tax bracket. This dollar amount is your tax savings—it costs you only $1,842 to max out on your contribution after factoring in the tax savings from your deduction for the contribution.

Caution

The new limits apply to retirement plans in 2002 only if "good faith" amendments are adopted before year-end; otherwise 2001 limits apply in 2002. The discussion assumes required amendments have been made.

butions are required for IRAs. Elective deferrals can be made to the following types of plans:

- 401(k) plans.
- 403(b) annuities.
- 457 government plans.
- Salary reduction simplified employee pensions (SARSEPs) established before 1997.
- SIMPLE plans.

Elective Deferral Limits

PLANS OTHER THAN SIMPLE PLANS. For 2002, the tax law has raised the elective deferral limit for all retirement plans (other than SIMPLE plans) to $11,000 (from $10,500 in 2001). This is called the "basic" elective deferral limit.

If you're age 50 or older by the end of 2002, there is an additional elective deferral limit, called a "catch-up amount," of $1,000. Thus, someone who is 55 in 2002 can agree to contribute up to $12,000 of salary to a 401(k) plan. This additional contribution amount was enacted to allow those who previously failed to make contributions—for example, women returning to the workforce after raising children who missed years of contribution opportunities—to make up for lost time. But, in operation, you do not have to show that you failed to make prior contributions. The *only* requirement for the additional catch-up amount is meeting the age 50 requirement.

PLANNING.   If you will celebrate your 50th birthday *during* the year, you can agree to make a catch-up contribution *throughout* the year; you don't have to wait until your birthday actually passes to start these additional elective deferrals.

For participants in 457 plans, there is a special limit for the three years prior to retirement. The limit during these three years is twice the otherwise applicable elective deferral limit. (See Example 2.)

How much can you contribute? The answer not only de-

Example 2

A state worker, age 59, is set to retire in three years at age 62. His contribution limit for 2002 is $24,000 ($11,000 basic plus $1,000 catch-up amount × 2).

pends on the new law limits (and what you can afford), but also on the terms of your plan. Under new law changes for 2002, you may be permitted to contribute up to 100 percent of your compensation to the plan (up to the applicable dollar limit). However, your employer plan may put a percentage limit on your contribution—for example, up to 5 percent of your annual compensation. Thus, if you earn $50,000, your limit under the terms of the plan may be only $2,500, even though the law provides an elective deferral limit for someone age 50 and older of $12,000.

As discussed earlier, in order for plans to allow you to take advantage of the new limits they must be amended to adopt these limits as well as eliminate self-imposed percentage limitations. Your plan administrator will advise you of your salary reduction options.

LOOKING AHEAD

The basic elective deferral amount for retirement plans *and* the catch-up amount are scheduled to increase in the future. Table 5.1 shows your elective deferral limits for plans other than SIMPLE plans (based on age) in the coming years.

TABLE 5.1 Elective Deferral Limits

Year	Limit for Those under Age 50	Limit for Those 50 and Older
2003	$12,000	$14,000
2004	13,000	16,000
2005	14,000	18,000
2006	15,000*	20,000*

*After 2006 the basic $15,000 limit and the additional $5,000 catch-up amount are each indexed for inflation in increments of $500.

LOOKING AHEAD

The basic elective deferral amount *and* the catch-up amount for SIMPLE plans are scheduled to increase in the future. Table 5.2 shows your elective deferral limits (based on age) after 2002.

SIMPLE PLANS. For 2002, the basic elective deferral limit for these plans has been raised to $7,000 (from $6,500 in 2001). In addition, there is a catch-up amount for those age 50 and older by year-end of $500. Thus in 2002 you can make an elective deferral contribution of up to $7,500.

IRA Limits

For 2002, you can contribute up to $3,000 to a traditional IRA or a Roth IRA. This is called the "basic" contribution limit.

If you're age 50 or older by the end of 2002, your contribution limit is $3,500. This is comprised of your basic contribution ($3,000) plus a catch-up contribution of $500. Eligibility is based solely on attaining the age of 50 by the

TABLE 5.2 Elective Deferral Limits for SIMPLE Plans

Year	Limit for Those under Age 50	Limit for Those 50 and Older
2003	$ 8,000	$ 9,000
2004	9,000	10,500
2005	10,000	12,000
2006	10,000*	12,500*

*After 2005 the basic $10,000 limit will be indexed for inflation in increments of $500. Starting in 2007, the additional $2,500 amount will also be indexed for inflation in increments of $500. Thus, the contribution limit in 2006 for those age 50 and older may be *more* than $12,500 (depending on inflation adjustments).

end of the year; it has nothing to do with whether you made contributions in the prior years.

For married couples, the additional catch-up contribution depends on the age of the IRA owner—not the contributor. (See Example 3.)

LOOKING AHEAD

The basic contribution limit *and* the catch-up contribution limit for IRAs for 2003 and 2004 are the same as in 2002. However, starting in 2005, they are scheduled to increase in the future. Table 5.3 shows your contribution limits (based on age).

Example 3

In 2002, Mary, age 48, works for XYZ Corp. Her husband Juan, age 51, is a full-time student who has no earnings. Mary may contribute only $3,000 to her own IRA, but she may contribute up to $3,500 to an IRA for Juan.

TABLE 5.3 IRA Contribution Limits

Year	Limit for Those under Age 50	Limit for Those 50 and Older
2003	$3,000	$3,500
2004	3,000	3,500
2005	4,000	4,500
2006	4,000	5,000
2007	4,000	5,000
2008 and thereafter	5,000*	6,000*

*The basic contribution limit will be adjusted for inflation in increments of $500, but there will be *no* adjustment to the additional contribution limit of $1,000.

ELIGIBILITY TO MAKE DEDUCTIBLE IRA CONTRIBUTIONS. If you are a participant in a qualified retirement plan, such as a company profit-sharing plan or pension plan, you can make deductible IRA contributions only if your modified AGI (MAGI) is below set limits. MAGI over a set limit causes the contribution to be phased out; it is fully phased out when MAGI exceeds another limit. The phaseout limits have increased for 2002 and are scheduled to increase further as outlined in Table 5.4 (without any indexing for inflation).

PLANNING. The interplay between the increasing IRA contribution limits on the one hand and the increasing phaseout limits on the other makes it highly complicated to determine your annual deductible contribution limit. Depending on changes in income and age, your limits may increase or decrease each year. (See Examples 4 and 5.)

TABLE 5.4 IRA Contribution Phaseout Limits

Year	Single Taxpayers	Joint Filers
2002	$34,000–$44,000	$54,000–$ 64,000
2003	40,000– 50,000	60,000– 70,000
2004	45,000– 55,000	65,000– 75,000
2005	50,000– 60,000	70,000– 80,000
2006	50,000– 60,000	75,000– 85,000
2007 and thereafter	50,000– 60,000	80,000– 100,000

Example 4

In 2002, Helen, a single individual, age 49, who participates in her company retirement plan wants to make deductible IRA contributions. Helen's MAGI is $39,000. Her deductible contribution limit is $1,500.

Example 5

In 2003, Helen's MAGI rises to $42,500. Her deductible contribution limit drops to $1,000 even though the potential deduction limit for 2003 increases from $3,000 to $3,500.

ELIGIBILITY TO MAKE ROTH IRA CONTRIBUTIONS. The income limits for making nondeductible Roth IRA contributions and for converting a traditional IRA to a Roth IRA remain unchanged for this year. Both limits are based on modified adjusted gross income (MAGI). For 2002, the limits are as follows:

- *Contribution phaseout limits:* $95,000 to $110,000 for singles and $150,000 to $160,000 for joint filers.
- *Conversion limits:* MAGI of $100,000 regardless of filing status (no conversion is allowed for a married person filing separately).

Planning for Higher Contribution Limits

While the higher contribution limits provide an excellent opportunity for you to save for your future retirement income, your current financial obligations may limit your ability to take full advantage of the opportunity. For instance, you may only be able to save $3,600 ($300 a month) in 2002. If this is so, then it's important for you to use your limited resources in the plan where they will produce the highest returns to you.

If you face the choice between making a contribution to your employer's 401(k) plan or funding a personal IRA, generally it's advisable to opt for the company plan. The reason: You can usually achieve more significant benefits.

- *Employer matching contributions.* These are essentially free additional retirement savings (although you will have to pay tax on this amount when you later take withdrawals). This benefit is improved by more rapid vesting requirements for employer contributions, discussed in the next subsection. However, not all plans provide employee matching contributions, so check with your plan administrator.

- *Creditor protection for funds in the plan.* If you experience serious financial difficulties, the funds in a company plan (both your contributions and employer contributions on your behalf) are fully protected from the claims of your creditors. In contrast, creditor protection for IRAs depends on state law (some states provide complete creditor protection while others provide limited or no protection for this asset).

MORE RAPID EMPLOYER VESTING. In some cases employers can or must make matching contributions with respect to employee elective deferrals. For example, employer matching of at least a certain amount is required for SIMPLE plans. And employers often make certain matching contributions to 401(k) plans in order to encourage rank-and-file employees to participate so that highly compensated employees can also make elective deferrals without causing the plan to be deemed discriminatory.

Starting in 2002, employer matching contributions vest more rapidly than in the past. Employers can opt for either of two vesting schedules:

- *Cliff vesting:* 100 percent vesting after three years. Prior to 2002 cliff vesting for these employer contributions could be delayed until five years.

- *Graded vesting:* 20 percent after two years, 40 percent after three years, 60 percent after four years, 80 percent after five years, and 100 percent vesting after six years. Prior to 2002 for employer matching contributions could be spread over seven years.

Note: The more rapid vesting schedule for employer matching contributions does not have to be used for other employer contributions to a qualified retirement plan.

WORKING COUPLES. If, as a couple, you have limited funds to contribute, it's important to coordinate where the family funds should be directed so that they'll do the greatest good. Consider the following factors if you have to make this important decision:

- *Eligibility for plan participation.* If each spouse is eligible to participate in a company plan, then decide which plan offers the greater benefit (factoring in employer matching contributions and investment options, discussed next). If only one spouse is eligible to participate in a plan, then decide whether funds should be directed to that plan or to IRAs.

- *Employer matching contributions.* Obviously contributions should be made where they'll earn the greater employer matching contributions. For example, if one spouse's plan has 3 percent matching and the other plan has 50 percent matching up to a set limit, the latter plan is probably a better option.

- *Investment options.* Under the law, 401(k) plans are required to provide a certain number of investment options. Compare the options under each plan. If you opt for an IRA, however, you obtain virtually an unlimited number of investment options by setting up a self-directed IRA.

Tax Credits for Making Contributions to Retirement Plans and IRAs

New tax credits encourage both individuals and employers to pay attention to retirement plans.

RETIREMENT SAVINGS CONTRIBUTIONS CREDIT. Low- and moderate-income individuals may be able to "double-dip"—that is, enjoy a tax benefit from making the contribution (such as a deduction for an IRA contribution or tax deferral on salary contributed to a 401(k) or SIMPLE plan) as well as claiming a new tax credit for the same contribution.

The credit is figured on contributions or elective deferrals up to $2,000. The amount of the credit is your applicable percentage—determined by your filing status and adjusted gross income, as shown in Table 5.5. (Also see Example 6.)

TABLE 5.5 Applicable Percentage for Retirement Savings Contribution Credit

Adjusted Gross Income						
Joint Filers		Heads of Household		Other Filers		
Over	Not Over	Over	Not Over	Over	Not Over	Applicable Percentage
$ 0	$30,000	$ 0	$22,500	$ 0	$15,000	50%
30,000	32,500	22,500	24,375	15,000	16,250	20
32,500	50,000	24,375	37,500	16,250	25,000	10
50,000		37,500		25,000		0

Example 6

In 2002, you contribute $6,000 of your salary to your company's 401(k) plan through elective deferrals. You are single and your adjusted gross income for the year is $24,000. In addition to *not* being immediately taxed on the $6,000 of salary you contributed to the plan, you can claim a tax credit of $200 (10 percent of $2,000, the maximum amount taken into account in figuring the credit). If your AGI is $25,001, you cannot claim any tax credit—as a single person your AGI exceeds the limit for the credit.

Caution

The contribution amount for purposes of figuring the tax credit is reduced by any distributions you take from a qualified plan that are includable in income during a "testing period." The contribution amount is also reduced by any Roth IRA rollover during the testing period that is not a qualified rollover.

The testing period includes the two preceding years, the current year, and the following year through the due date of the return (including extensions). Thus, for purposes of figuring the credit for 2002, consider whether any distributions were taken in 2000, 2001, 2002, and up to April 15, 2003 (assuming there are no filing extensions obtained).

LOOKING AHEAD

The retirement savings contribution credit is set to run only through 2006. The percentages, AGI limits, and $2,000 maximum amount taken into account in figuring the credit will *not* be adjusted for inflation in the coming years.

PLANNING. You must weigh very carefully whether to take withdrawals—for example, IRA withdrawals to pay for the purchase of your first home or to cover medical or educational expenses. Distributions can be taken for certain purposes without incurring the 10 percent penalty on early withdrawals if you are under age $59\frac{1}{2}$, but they may cost you the credit (in addition to ordinary income taxes on the distributions).

EMPLOYER CREDIT FOR STARTING A RETIREMENT PLAN. Small businesses may be eligible for a new tax credit designed to encourage starting up a qualified retirement plan. The credit covers the administrative costs of plan setup and employee education and runs for the first three years of the plan's existence. This credit is explained in greater detail in Chapter 6.

Required Minimum Distribution Rules

The tax law does not allow funds to remain in qualified retirement plans and IRAs indefinitely, building up income that isn't currently taxed. At a certain point you *must* take distributions from your retirement accounts—at least enough to avoid penalties. This amount is referred to as your annual required minimum distribution.

In 2002, final regulations on figuring minimum distributions were released. These regulations provide highly favorable rules that effectively have lower requirements than under prior rules, allowing you to leave funds in retirement accounts to build up on a tax-deferred basis if you do not need to withdraw the money for retirement income. The final regulations generally become effective *after* 2002, but you can opt to use them to figure minimum distributions in 2002 (for qualified plans they can be used in 2002 only if the plan is amended to include them). Alternatively, you may use the rules created by proposed regulations issued in 2001 or proposed regulations issued in 1987. The following discussion details distribution rules based on the final regulations. For most taxpayers these rules will prove to be the best choice for minimizing distribution requirements and avoiding penalties.

Lifetime Required Minimum Distributions

While many of the basic rules remain unchanged, new for 2002 are revised tables used to figure distributions. These tables reflect new mortality figures; since people are living longer, the amount required to be distributed each year is smaller under these new tables than under previous IRS tables.

GENERAL RULE. Your required minimum distribution is your account balance as of December 31 of the prior year divided by the distribution period specified in the new Uniform Lifetime Table. (See Table 5.6.) This distribution period assumes you've named a beneficiary who is 10 years younger than you, regardless of whether in fact you named any beneficiary and, if so, whether that beneficiary is younger or even older than you. (See Examples 7 and 8.)

YOUNGER SPOUSE. If you've named your spouse as the sole beneficiary of your account or benefits *and* your spouse is

---

Example 7

You attain age 70½ in February 2002 and reach your 71st birthday in August of the same year. Your IRA account balance on December 31, 2001, was $100,000. You take your first distribution on December 31, 2002. Using the Uniform Lifetime Table, your required minimum distribution is $3,774 ($100,000 ÷ 26.5).

TABLE 5.6 Uniform Lifetime Table

Age of Employee	Distribution Period
70	27.4
71	26.5
72	25.6
73	24.7
74	23.8
75	22.9
76	22.0
77	21.2
78	20.3
79	19.5
80	18.7
81	17.9
82	17.1
83	16.3
84	15.5
85	14.8
86	14.1
87	13.4
88	12.7
89	12.0
90	11.4
91	10.8
92	10.2

(Continued)

TABLE 5.6 *(Continued)*

Age of Employee	Distribution Period
93	9.6
94	9.1
95	8.6
96	8.1
97	7.6
98	7.1
99	6.7
100	6.3
101	5.9
102	5.5
103	5.2
104	4.9
105	4.5
106	4.2
107	3.9
108	3.7
109	3.4
110	3.1
111	2.9
112	2.6
113	2.4
114	2.1
115+	1.9

Example 8

On December 31, 2002, your account balance is $101,226 ($100,000 + 5% earnings during year – $3,774 distribution). Using the new distribution period from the Uniform Lifetime Table, your minimum distribution for 2003 is $3,954 ($101,226 ÷ 25.6).

more than 10 years your junior, instead of using the Uniform Lifetime Table to find the distribution period, you use the Joint Life and Last Survivor Expectancy Table. (See Table 5.7.) Doing so provides a smaller distribution than would be required under the Uniform Lifetime Table. Marital status for purposes of figuring your distribution for the year is determined on the first day of the year, so any changes in that status due to death or divorce are ignored. (See Example 9.)

Example 9

Same as Example 7 except you've named your spouse, who turned age 60 in 2002, as the sole beneficiary of your IRA. Using the Joint Life and Last Survivor Expectancy Table, your minimum distribution for 2002 is $3,676 ($100,000 ÷ 27.2). This is about $100 less than if your spouse were not more than 10 years your junior.

TABLE 5.7 Joint Life and Last Survivor Expectancy Table

	70	71	72	73	74	75	76	77	78	79	80	81	82	83	84	85
52	33.4	33.3	33.2	33.1	33.0	33.0	32.9	32.8	32.8	32.7	32.7	32.6	32.6	32.6	32.5	32.5
53	32.6	32.5	32.4	32.3	32.2	32.1	32.0	32.0	31.0	31.8	31.8	31.8	31.7	31.7	31.7	31.6
54	31.8	31.7	31.6	31.5	31.4	31.3	31.2	31.1	31.0	31.0	30.9	30.9	30.8	30.8	30.8	30.7
55	31.1	30.9	30.8	30.6	30.5	30.4	30.3	30.3	30.2	30.1	30.1	30.0	30.0	29.9	29.9	29.9
56	30.3	30.1	30.0	29.8	29.7	29.6	29.5	29.4	29.3	29.3	29.2	29.2	29.1	29.1	29.0	29.0
57	29.5	29.4	29.2	29.1	28.9	28.8	28.7	28.6	28.5	28.4	28.4	28.3	28.3	28.2	28.2	28.1
58	28.8	28.6	28.4	28.3	28.1	28.0	27.9	27.8	27.7	27.6	27.5	27.5	27.4	27.4	27.3	27.3
59	28.1	27.9	27.7	27.5	27.4	27.2	27.1	27.0	26.9	26.8	26.7	26.6	26.6	26.5	26.5	26.4
60	27.4	27.2	27.0	26.8	26.6	26.5	26.3	26.2	26.1	26.0	25.9	25.8	25.8	25.7	25.6	25.6
61	26.7	26.5	26.3	26.1	25.9	25.7	25.6	25.4	25.3	25.2	25.1	25.0	24.9	24.9	24.8	24.8
62	26.1	25.8	25.6	25.4	25.2	25.0	24.8	24.7	24.6	24.4	24.3	24.2	24.1	24.1	24.0	23.9
63	25.4	25.2	24.9	24.7	24.5	24.3	24.1	23.9	23.8	23.7	23.6	23.4	23.4	23.3	23.2	23.1
64	24.8	24.5	24.3	24.0	23.8	23.6	23.4	23.2	23.1	22.9	22.8	22.7	22.6	22.5	22.4	22.3
65	24.3	23.9	23.7	23.4	23.1	22.9	22.7	22.5	22.4	22.2	22.1	21.9	21.8	21.7	21.6	21.6
66	23.7	23.4	23.1	22.8	22.5	22.3	22.0	21.8	21.7	21.5	21.3	21.2	21.1	21.0	20.9	20.8
67	23.2	22.8	22.5	22.2	21.9	21.6	21.4	21.2	21.0	20.8	20.6	20.5	20.4	20.2	20.1	20.1
68	22.7	22.3	22.0	21.6	21.3	21.0	20.8	20.6	20.3	20.1	20.0	19.8	19.7	19.5	19.4	19.3
69	22.2	21.8	21.4	21.1	20.8	20.5	20.2	19.9	19.7	19.5	19.3	19.1	19.0	18.8	18.7	18.6
70	21.8	21.3	20.9	20.6	20.2	19.9	19.6	19.4	19.1	18.9	18.7	18.5	18.3	18.2	18.0	17.9
71	21.3	20.9	20.5	20.1	19.7	19.4	19.1	18.8	18.5	18.3	18.1	17.9	17.7	17.5	17.4	17.3
72	20.9	20.5	20.0	19.6	19.3	18.9	18.6	18.3	18.0	17.7	17.5	17.3	17.1	16.9	16.7	16.6
73	20.6	20.1	19.6	19.2	18.8	18.4	18.1	17.8	17.5	17.2	16.9	16.7	16.5	16.3	16.1	16.0
74	20.2	19.7	19.3	18.8	18.4	18.0	17.6	17.3	17.0	16.7	16.4	16.2	15.9	15.7	15.5	15.4
75	19.9	19.4	18.9	18.4	18.0	17.6	17.2	16.8	16.5	16.2	15.9	15.6	15.4	15.2	15.0	14.8
76	19.6	19.1	18.6	18.1	17.6	17.2	16.8	16.4	16.0	15.7	15.4	15.1	14.9	14.7	14.4	14.3
77	19.4	18.8	18.3	17.8	17.3	16.8	16.4	16.0	15.6	15.3	15.0	14.7	14.4	14.2	13.9	13.7
78	19.1	18.5	18.0	17.5	17.0	16.5	16.0	15.6	15.2	14.9	14.5	14.2	13.9	13.7	13.4	13.2
79	18.9	18.3	17.7	17.2	16.7	16.2	15.7	15.3	14.9	14.5	14.1	13.8	13.5	13.2	13.0	12.8

Note: For additional life expectancy factors, refer to the Supplement to IRS Publication 590, "Individual Retirement Arrangements."

OTHER CHANGES ON DISTRIBUTION COMPUTATIONS. For the year you attain age $70\frac{1}{2}$ you can opt to take your first distribution by April 1 of the following year instead of December 31 of that year. This rule has *not* been changed by the final regulations. But the way you figure your second distribution has been changed. If you opt to delay the first distribution until April 1 of the year after turning age $70\frac{1}{2}$, then for purposes of figuring your second distribution on December 31 of the year you turn $71\frac{1}{2}$ (the same year in which you take your first one), you need *not* reduce the account balance by the first distribution—you simply divide the account balance on December 31 by your distribution period for the second year. This new rule eliminates the need to reduce the account balance by the first distribution, simplifying your computations. However, it results in a slightly larger second distribution. (See Example 10.)

PLANNING. If you've already started taking required distributions, you can switch to the new rules for 2002 (you *must* switch in 2003). Doing so will, in most situations, result in smaller distributions than under the prior rules. Perhaps the

Example 10

Same as Example 7 except that instead of taking your first distribution on December 31, 2002, you postpone it until April 1, 2003. Your second distribution (taken on December 31, 2003) is $4,101 ($105,000 ÷ 25.6).

only situation in which using prior rules produces a more favorable result is for beneficiaries of individuals who died after their required beginning date and were figuring their minimum distributions before death using the old term certain method under the 1987 proposed regulations (post-death distributions are discussed later in this chapter). Such beneficiaries have smaller minimums for 2002 if they continue to use the old rules—but they *must* use the new rules for 2003 and later years.

Reporting for Required Minimum Distributions

There is no reporting—to you or to the IRS—in 2002. However, starting in 2003, trustees and custodians will be required to inform owners by January 31 of their need to take minimum distributions during the year. They must also offer to compute the amount for the owner (but they aren't required to make the computation automatically). It is generally expected that in the coming years (perhaps not as soon as 2003), trustees and custodians will routinely provide owners with their required distribution amounts.

Starting in 2004, IRA trustees and custodians will report to the IRS each account for which a distribution was required in the prior year (but not the amount paid out). Thus, the 2004 notices to the IRS will concern 2003 distributions.

Postdeath Distributions

If you inherit retirement plan benefits or an IRA, the receipt of the inheritance is initially income tax free, but receipt of the benefits themselves (such as withdrawals from IRA accounts) is taxable because the funds have never been taxed. How soon you dip into your inheritance depends on your personal financial needs *and* on required minimum distribution rules. You can withdraw the funds all at once from an inherited IRA. There is no early distribution penalty even if you are (or the person you inherited the account from was) under age 59½. The extent of withdrawals of benefits permitted from qualified plans depends on the terms of those plans (the plan administrator can inform you of your options).

Assuming you don't need the funds immediately, you still must take certain distributions in order to avoid penalties on underwithdrawals. The amount depends on whether death occurred before or after the owner had begun distributions and whether there is a "designated beneficiary" for the benefits or the IRA.

The determination of who is the designated beneficiary must be made no later than September 30 of the year following the year of the owner's death. The determination is based on who was named as a beneficiary before the owner's death and whether any such beneficiary is still alive and, if so, has disclaimed an interest or "cashed out" his/her benefit by this date (explained later in this chapter). If benefits are payable to the owner's estate or to a charity, there is no designated beneficiary—anyone receiving these benefits must take them in full no later than the end of the fifth year following the year of death if the owner died before the required beginning date or over the owner's remaining life expectancy (ignoring the fact that he or she is dead) if the owner died after the required beginning date. (See Example 11.)

Example 11

Dad, who was predeceased by Mom, died in 2002. The benefits in his IRA pass to his estate because he never changed the beneficiary designation from Mom to someone else or named a successor/contingent beneficiary and, under the terms of the account, benefits are automatically payable to the owner's estate. Under the terms of Dad's will, Junior inherits everything in the estate. For purposes of figuring required distributions, there is no designated beneficiary—benefits are payable to the estate. Thus, even though Junior has the right to the benefits, he is *not* the designated beneficiary so he must withdraw *all* of the funds no later than December 31, 2007, the last day of the fifth year following the year of Dad's death.

SURVIVING SPOUSE. As under prior rules, if a surviving spouse inherits an IRA, she may roll over the benefits to her own IRA. This will enable her not only to make contributions to the account if eligible to do so but also to postpone any distribution until her required beginning date—the year in which she turns age $70\frac{1}{2}$.

The election to make the rollover can be done at any time after the IRA owner's death by *not* taking a distribution as described below or by contributing to the account. As a practical matter, the election is really made by changing the title of the account into the name of the surviving spouse. If funds are distributed to the surviving spouse (and they're not a required distribution), the survivor can roll them over to her IRA within 60 days of the distribution.

The death of the owner does not eliminate the need to take the owner's required minimum distribution for the year. Thus the amount eligible to be rolled over to a surviving spouse's IRA must be reduced by the owner's last distribution.

OWNER DIES ON OR AFTER THE REQUIRED BEGINNING DATE. If there is a designated beneficiary, generally he or she must take distributions over his or her life expectancy (based on the Single Life Table). (See Table 5.8 and Examples 12 and 13.)

However, the beneficiary may opt to take distributions over the owner's remaining life expectancy. If the beneficiary is older than the owner at the time of death (for example, the owner designated his older sister as the beneficiary of his IRA), the option to use the owner's remaining life expectancy will result in a smaller required distribution.

If there is no designated beneficiary (for example, the funds are left to the owner's estate), distributions are figured using the owner's age on his/her birthday during the year of death. Each year thereafter, the life expectancy is simply reduced by one.

OWNER DIES BEFORE THE REQUIRED BEGINNING DATE. If there is a designated beneficiary, he or she must take distributions over his or her life expectancy (based on the Single Life Table) *unless* the IRA trustee requires or allows the beneficiary to elect to use the five-year rule (i.e., complete distribution by the end of the fifth year following the year of death).

If there is no designated beneficiary, the account must be distributed by the end of the fifth year following the year of death.

TABLE 5.8 Single Life Table

Age	Life Expectancy	Age	Life Expectancy
0	82.4	22	61.1
1	81.6	23	60.1
2	80.6	24	59.1
3	79.7	25	58.2
4	78.7	26	57.2
5	77.7	27	56.2
6	76.7	28	55.3
7	75.8	29	54.3
8	74.8	30	53.3
9	73.8	31	52.4
10	72.8	32	51.4
11	71.8	33	50.4
12	70.8	34	49.4
13	69.9	35	48.5
14	68.9	36	47.5
15	67.9	37	46.5
16	66.9	38	45.6
17	66.0	39	44.6
18	65.0	40	43.6
19	64.0	41	42.7
20	63.0	42	41.7
21	62.1	43	40.7

TABLE 5.8 *(Continued)*

Age	Life Expectancy	Age	Life Expectancy
44	39.8	66	20.2
45	38.8	67	19.4
46	37.9	68	18.6
47	37.0	69	17.8
48	36.0	70	17.0
49	35.1	71	16.3
50	34.2	72	15.5
51	33.3	73	14.8
52	32.3	74	14.1
53	31.4	75	13.4
54	30.5	76	12.7
55	29.6	77	12.1
56	28.7	78	11.4
57	27.9	79	10.8
58	27.0	80	10.2
59	26.1	81	9.7
60	25.2	82	9.1
61	24.4	83	8.6
62	23.5	84	8.1
63	22.7	85	7.6
64	21.8	86	7.1
65	21.0	87	6.7

(Continued)

TABLE 5.8 *(Continued)*

Age	Life Expectancy	Age	Life Expectancy
88	6.3	100	2.9
89	5.9	101	2.7
90	5.5	102	2.5
91	5.2	103	2.3
92	4.9	104	2.1
93	4.6	105	1.9
94	4.3	106	1.7
95	4.1	107	1.5
96	3.8	108	1.4
97	3.6	109	1.2
98	3.4	110	1.1
99	3.1	111+	1.0

Example 12

An IRA owner dies in 2002 when he is 77 years old. His 73-year-old sister is the beneficiary of the account. She figures her minimum distribution based on her life expectancy from the Single Life Table. Her distribution for 2002 is the account balance divided by 14.8.

Example 13

A beneficiary does not recalculate life expectancy each year but merely reduces the initial life expectancy by one. Thus, for 2003, the sister's minimum distribution is the account balance divided by 13.8 (14.8 – 1).

PUTTING THE NEW RULES INTO EFFECT FOR EXISTING HEIRS. If, as a beneficiary, you had opted to use the five-year rule, you can now change to taking distributions over your life expectancy if you act by December 31, 2003, or by the end of the fifth year following the year of the owner's death.

The final regulations require that you look back in time to redetermine whether there was a designated beneficiary and who that beneficiary was. In effect, you must look back to September 30 of the year following the IRA owner's death. This redetermination can impact your required distributions—positively or negatively, depending on the circumstances. Unfortunately, there is nothing you can do to alter the results at this time; you may be forced to take more rapid distributions than you had in the past if either of the following two situations occur:

- The original designated beneficiary died after the required beginning date but before the death of the IRA owner. For example, assume that an IRA owner started taking distributions in 1997 when he turned age $70\frac{1}{2}$. His 45-year-old son was the designated beneficiary, but he died in 1998. The IRA owner never named a contingent beneficiary and died in 1999. Under the old rules, distributions could continue to be paid out over the son's life expectancy in 1997 (when the distributions began). But under the new rules, starting in 2003, the account must be paid out over the IRA owner's remaining life expectancy since there was no designated beneficiary on September 30, 2000.

- The original designated beneficiary disclaimed his interest in the IRA and no contingent beneficiary was named. Again, in this case, the account balance must be paid out over the IRA owner's remaining life expectancy.

BENEFICIARY PLANNING. In light of the new required minimum distribution rules, it's important for you to review your beneficiary designations. And if you are named as a beneficiary (or a contingent beneficiary) be sure to take appropriate actions no later than September 30 following the year of the IRA owner's death if desirable.

BENEFICIARY DESIGNATIONS. Make sure that you've not only named a beneficiary for your IRA and retirement plan benefits, but also provided for a contingent (successor) beneficiary who becomes the designated beneficiary if that person is not alive on September 30 of the year following the year of your death. Keep a copy of all your beneficiary designation forms with your important papers; don't rely on your IRA custodian to do so because these forms can easily be lost (for example, if your IRA custodian is a bank, the forms can be lost upon a merger with another bank).

In making your designations, keep in mind who is or is not considered a designated beneficiary. An estate and a charitable organization may be named as a beneficiary to inherit an IRA or a part of one. But, since they have no life expectancy, they are not considered designated beneficiaries. Nonetheless you may still wish to name them as beneficiaries—to provide liquidity for your estate if the estate is the beneficiary or to benefit your favorite charity if that charity is the beneficiary.

✳ You may name a trust—either revocable or irrevocable— as the beneficiary of your IRA. In this instance, all trust beneficiaries are viewed as the designated beneficiaries of your IRA, so distributions are figured using the life expectancy of the oldest beneficiary. For this purpose, trust beneficiaries include both those with a life interest and those with a remainder interest. Trust beneficiaries do not include a trust's contingent beneficiaries.

You must provide the IRA custodian or trustee with certain documents, including a copy of the trust. The failure to do so will result in there being *no* designated beneficiary, so that the opportunity to stretch out required minimum distributions over a trust beneficiary's life expectancy will be lost. *Note:* Trusts that failed in the past to provide this paperwork to the IRA custodian or trustee have a grace period to correct the deficiency: They must act by October 31, 2003, to provide all necessary documents.

If you have a single IRA, you may wish to divide your account and name separate beneficiaries for each. This will allow each beneficiary to take distributions over his or her life expectancy. If multiple beneficiaries are named to one account, then the life of the oldest beneficiary (with the shortest life expectancy) is used to figure postdeath distributions. Of course, the beneficiaries can opt to subdivide the account after your death, but if you do it, you'll avoid any problems your beneficiaries may encounter.

POSTDEATH ACTIONS. There are several actions that can be taken after an IRA owner's death to affect required minimum distributions.

- *Disclaimers.* A designated beneficiary may disclaim his or her interest, allowing it to pass to a contingent beneficiary. The disclaimer must be valid under federal law (i.e., a written disclaimer made no later than nine months after the death of the IRA owner, disclaiming any interest before any benefits have been accepted). A disclaimer can be used effectively, for example, to pass benefits to a younger beneficiary so that the required distributions will be stretched out over a longer period of time. An estate may *not* disclaim the inheritance in order to create a designated beneficiary for the IRA.
- *Cash-outs.* A portion of benefits can be paid *before* the September 30 deadline. This option can be used to remove a charity as beneficiary so that remaining individuals can use their life expectancies to figure minimum distributions.
- *Account divisions.* A single IRA with multiple beneficiaries can be divided into separate accounts for each beneficiary. This will allow each beneficiary to take dis-

tributions over his or her own life expectancy. It will also allow each beneficiary to make investment decisions independent from the other beneficiaries.

Other Retirement Planning Changes

Employer-Paid Retirement Planning Advice

If your employer pays for retirement planning advice for you and your spouse to help you figure out what you need to save for retirement and what distribution you need to take from your personal IRAs as well as company retirement plans, you are not taxed on this fringe benefit. As of 2002, it is excludable from your income if the employer maintains a qualified retirement plan such as a 401(k) plan and provides the advice or information on a nondiscriminatory basis (that is, the benefit is not limited to owners or executives but available to all employees).

There is no dollar limit on this exclusion. However, it does not apply to certain related services, such as tax preparation, accounting, legal, or brokerage services. If your employer also pays for these services, you are taxed on the value of those benefits.

Roth IRA Conversions

The rules for converting a traditional IRA to a Roth IRA have not changed in 2002. The income limit on eligibility to make the conversion continues to be MAGI of no more than $100,000. This figure is *not* adjusted annually for inflation.

However, an important ruling in 2002 may prove helpful to those who attempted to make a conversion only to find out after having done so that they were in fact ineligible for conversion. Generally, you have until October 15 of the year following the year of conversion to recharacterize the transaction (i.e., retitle the Roth IRA as a traditional IRA) in order to avoid having the account treated as a taxable distribution (and subject to penalty if you're under age $59\frac{1}{2}$).

But the IRS says you may have an even longer time to recharacterize the account in special circumstances. In one instance a taxpayer learned two years after the conversion that income has been omitted through no fault of his. The IRS gave him an additional six months to recharacterize the Roth IRA as a traditional IRA.

Caution

While this IRS grace was expressed in a private letter ruling that technically can't be relied on as precedent by another taxpayer, it serves to illustrate an option open to you if you find yourself in similar circumstances: Ask the IRS to grant you additional time to recharacterize an erroneously converted account.

CHAPTER 6

Small Business Tax Relief

With the economy sagging in the past several years, Congress has created a number of tax incentives designed to spur businesses to make capital investments and to hire new workers. Presumably, if businesses act on these incentives, they will put more money back into the economy, thereby making it grow.

This chapter covers the new incentives for small business. Some of the incentives are new or expanded deductions. Others are income deferral mechanisms, and still others are tax credits. This chapter also discusses other small business tax changes enacted in prior years that take effect in 2002.

Incentives for New Equipment Purchases

Businesses can recoup the cost of equipment they purchase through special write-off allowances. In some cases, the write-off is immediate (such as first-year expensing), while in other cases the write-off must be taken over several years (such as depreciation). Law changes combine to allow for faster write-offs of investments in equipment.

First-Year Expensing

A small business can elect to expense the cost of equipment—computers, office furniture, machinery, and so on—instead of depreciating the cost over time, typically five to seven years. This is sometimes referred to as the Section 179 deduction because this is the section in the Internal Revenue Code governing the rule.

There is a set dollar limit on the amount that can be expensed annually. For 2002, that limit generally is $24,000. The same dollar limit applies where you pay cash or finance your equipment purchase over time.

The dollar limit phases out once a business' annual equipment purchases exceed $200,000. For every dollar over $200,000, the expense limit is reduced by $1, so that once equipment purchases exceed $224,000 in 2002, no expensing is permitted.

PLANNING. To make the most of expensing when more than $24,000 has been spent on equipment, it is advisable to elect expensing for the property with the longest depreciation recovery period. (See Example 1.)

LIBERTY ZONE BUSINESSES. Businesses in New York City affected by the terrorist attack on September 11, 2001, may be eligible for a higher expensing limit of $59,000 (the basic $24,000 limit plus an additional

LOOKING AHEAD

The dollar limit for equipment expensing for 2003 is set to increase to $25,000. However, there have been proposals to increase this limit even further (for example, to $30,000 or more), so stay alert to possible Congressional action.

$35,000 limit). This higher limit applies to so-called "Liberty Zone property." This is property placed in service after September 10, 2001, and before January 1, 2007, and used in a business within the Liberty Zone—the area south of Canal Street in Manhattan.

There is a special phaseout of the dollar limit for Liberty Zone property. Instead of the dollar-for-dollar reduction in the over $200,000 limit for excess purchases ($59,000),

---

Example 1

Company A spends $40,000 in 2002 on the following equipment: a $15,000 machine with a seven-year recovery period, $12,000 in office furniture with a seven-year recovery period, and $5,000 for a copier with a five-year recovery period. It is advisable to elect expensing for the $15,000 machine and $9,000 of the $12,000 in office furniture. This will leave only $3,000 that will be depreciated over seven years and $5,000 over five years.

LOOKING AHEAD

The dollar limit for Liberty Zone property placed in service in 2003 increases to $60,000 ($25,000 basic expensing plus $35,000 additional expensing). Thus, in 2003 the phaseout of expensing is completed when equipment purchases exceed $520,000.

there is only a 50 percent reduction. More precisely, the dollar limit is reduced by 50 percent of the cost of all Liberty Zone property over $200,000 so that in 2002 a business in the Liberty Zone does not lose the expensing opportunity until total purchases exceed $518,000 (instead of $224,000). (See Example 2.)

Bonus Depreciation

A new concept called bonus depreciation applies to property purchased after September 10, 2001, and before Sep-

---

Example 2

In 2002, a New York City corporation placed in service in the Liberty Zone one machine costing $65,000 as well as other Liberty Zone property costing $420,000. The maximum expense deduction is $16,500, figured as follows:

$65,000 + $420,000 = $485,000 (total Liberty Zone property)
$485,000 × 50% = $242,500
$242,500 − $200,000 = $42,500
$59,000 (maximum expense deduction) − $42,500 = $16,500
    (expense deduction)

---

tember 11, 2004, and placed in service before January 1, 2005. This write-off is in addition to any first-year expensing that may be claimed. Bonus depreciation may be claimed by any business, not merely one affected by the events of September 11.

Bonus depreciation is 30 percent of the adjusted basis of the property. Generally this is the cost of the property minus any first-year expensing (but special rules not discussed here apply to New York Liberty Zone property). (See Example 3.)

Bonus depreciation is designed merely to accelerate the write-off for equipment. It does not increase the total write-offs that may be claimed, which continue to be limited to the property's basis (generally cost). Table 6.1 contrasts the write-offs for five-year property with a cost $30,000 (assuming *no* first-year expensing election) using and not using bonus depreciation.

Example 3

On February 1, 2002, Company B buys equipment for $30,000. It elects to claim the maximum expense deduction of $24,000. It may also deduct $1,800 in bonus depreciation (30% × [$30,000 – $24,000]). The remaining basis of $4,200 ($30,000 – [$24,000 + $1,800]) may be depreciated over the property's recovery period. So, for example, if it is five-year property (assuming the half-year convention), the depreciation allowance for 2002 is $840 (20 percent of the $4,200). In total, Company B may deduct $26,640 of the $30,000 cost in 2002.

TABLE 6.1 Using Bonus Depreciation

Recovery Year	With Bonus Depreciation	Without Bonus Depreciation
2002	$13,200	$ 6,000
2003	6,720	9,600
2004	4,032	5,760
2005	2,419	3,456
2006	2,419	3,456
2007	1,210	1,728
Total depreciation	$30,000	$30,000

QUALIFYING PROPERTY. Most types of depreciable property qualify for 30 percent bonus depreciation. For example, it may be claimed for software that has a three-year recovery period. Bonus depreciation also applies to qualified leasehold improvement property—improvements to the interior of non-residential property made under a lease by the lessee, sublessee, or lessor. Further, it applies to property elected to be depreciated under the alternative depreciation system (ADS).

Nonqualifying property includes the following items:

- Intangibles (e.g., trademarks and goodwill) required to be amortized over 15 years.

- Property that *must* be depreciated under the alternative depreciation system, such as cell phones and other listed property not used more than 50 percent for business and any property used predominantly outside the United States.

- Property with a recovery period of over 20 years, such as residential realty (27.5 years) and nonresidential realty (39 years) other than qualified household improvements.

OTHER RULES. Bonus depreciation is not taken into account in determining the basis of property for purposes of the midquarter convention. Thus, the basis of property placed in service in the last quarter of the year is determined without regard to bonus depreciation. (See Example 4.)

ELECTING OUT OF BONUS DEPRECIATION. Although bonus depreciation is not *required* to be claimed, it applies unless you elect out of it. Generally, an election out is advisable where current income is not enough to benefit from the added write-off but you expect income to improve in coming years.

The election out applies to all property within the same recovery class. Thus, if you want bonus depreciation to apply to some five-year property, it must apply to all five-year property. By the same token, if you want to elect out of bonus depreciation for some seven-year property, the election out prohibits bonus depreciation for any other seven-year property.

Example 4

In February 2002, Company C places in service equipment costing $30,000. In December 2002, the company places in service more equipment costing $20,000. The determination of whether the midquarter convention applies to these items is based on the cost of the items without regard to any bonus depreciation.

The election out of bonus depreciation is made on Form 4652, Depreciation and Amortization. It must be made no later than the due date of the return (including extensions) for the year the property is placed in service (for example, by April 15, 2003, plus any filing extensions, for 2002 property).

Caution

If you want to make the election out of bonus depreciation but fail to do so properly, you must reduce the property's basis by the amount that you could have claimed as bonus depreciation, even if you didn't take the deduction. This will affect the amount of your gain (or loss), including depreciation recapture, when you dispose of the property.

Incentives for Business Cars

Whether you buy or lease a car for business, special rules govern how much you can deduct and when. For certain fuel-efficient cars, you may even qualify for an extra deduction or a special tax credit.

Dollar Limits on Car Deductions

If you buy a car, van, or light truck used in business, you can deduct your actual costs, including an allowance for depreciation or first-year expensing. However, there is a dollar limit on depreciation write-offs for "luxury cars" (vehicles costing over a set amount) weighing less than 6,000 pounds.

Alert: The IRS is considering a change in the rules to allow small trucks and vans to escape the dollar limits. Vehicles with limited opportunities for personal use (e.g., delivery vans that seat only a driver and one passenger) would qualify for exemption from the dollar limits. Stay alert as to when such a change would become effective.

For cars placed in service after September 11, 2001, and before January 1, 2005, the first-year dollar limit is increased by $4,600. Table 6.2 shows the dollar limits for cars placed in service in 2002.

The dollar limit without the additional amount effectively applies to cars costing more than $15,300. With the addition of the $4,600, the dollar limit does not start to apply until the cost of the car exceeds $17,409.

The full dollar limit applies only to cars used 100 percent for business. If you use your car 75 percent for business and 25 percent for personal purposes, you must allocate the dollar limit. (See Example 5.)

LOOKING AHEAD

The dollar limits on depreciation deductions for cars may be adjusted for inflation in 2003. However, the additional first-year dollar limit of $4,600 will not be adjusted for inflation.

TABLE 6.2 Business Deduction Dollar Limit for Cars Placed in Service in 2002

Year	Dollar Limit
2002	$7,660 ($3,060 + $4,600)
2003	4,900
2004	2,950
2005 and later years	1,775

Example 5

You buy a $22,000 car in 2002. (Assume the car weighs under 6,000 pounds.) You use it 75 percent for business and 25 percent for personal reasons. The most you can deduct in the first year of car ownership is $5,745 ($7,660 × 75%).

Standard Mileage Rate

Instead of deducting your actual expenses for the business use of your car, you can opt to claim an IRS standard mileage allowance. This standard mileage rate applies to both owned and leased cars used for business. The standard mileage rate takes the place of deducting gas and oil, insurance, depreciation on purchased cars (or lease payments on leased cars), and repairs and maintenance. For 2002, the standard mileage rate is 36.5 cents per mile (up from 34.5 cents per mile in 2001).

Although, as mentioned earlier, this rate may be claimed whether you own or lease the car, it may *not* be claimed if you deducted actual expenses for the car in a prior year.

DEEMED DEPRECIATION. If you claim the standard mileage rate, you must reduce the basis of your car by a deemed depreciation amount. The reduction in basis is necessary for determining how long to claim the standard mileage rate (it cannot be claimed after the car has been fully depreciated according to deemed depreciation). The basis reduction is also necessary for determining gain or loss on the sale of the car. For 2002, the deemed depreciation rate is 15 cents per mile (the same as the rate in 2001). (See Example 6.)

PLANNING. If you buy or lease a car for business in 2002, decide whether it's better to use the actual expense method or the IRS standard mileage rate to deduct the car's operating costs. Remember that the standard mileage rate replaces write-offs for depreciation (or lease costs on leased cars), gas, oil, repairs, licenses, and insurance. If you use the standard mileage rate in the first year you can switch to the actual expense method in a subsequent year; but you are limited to claiming straight-line depreciation if you own the car (no accelerated depreciation is permitted). Again, if you use the actual expense method in the first year you cannot later switch to the standard mileage rate.

The choice of which method to select depends on a couple of factors:

- *Records for actual costs.* Using the standard mileage rate eliminates the need to keep receipts for gas, oil, and so forth. It does not eliminate the requirement to

Example 6

You buy a $22,000 car in 2002. You drive it 35,000 miles on business. You must reduce the basis of the car by $5,250 (35,000 × $.15). Assuming the deemed depreciation rate remains unchanged in the coming years, your car will be fully depreciated within four years—and no additional standard mileage rate may be claimed afterward.

substantiate business use of the car (noting odometer readings for business use).

- *Number of miles.* The more you drive, the greater the standard mileage rate deduction proves to be, even for modestly priced cars since the same rate applies regardless of the car's sticker price. For example, if a car is driven 40,000 miles for business in 2002, the deduction under the standard mileage rate is $14,600. This same deduction applies if the car is a modestly priced Saturn or an expensive Mercedes.

Leased Cars

In order to roughly equate the write-offs allowed for leased cars with cars that are owned and depreciated, a special amount must be added back to income for leased cars. This is called an "inclusion amount." For 2002, it applies when the original cost of the car exceeds $15,500. Table 6.3 shows the inclusion amounts for cars (other than electric cars) first placed in service in 2002. These inclusion amounts are nearly half of the amounts in 2001, making it less costly—taxwise—to lease a business car in 2002 than it was in 2001. (Also see Example 7.)

Example 7

You lease a car in January 2002 that is worth $35,000. For 2002, the first year of the lease, you must add to income $89. In 2003, the inclusion amount is $196.

TABLE 6.3 Inclusion Amounts for Nonelectric Cars First Leased in 2002

Fair Market Value		Tax Year during Lease				
Over	Not Over	1st	2nd	3rd	4th	Later
$ 15,500	$ 15,800	$ 2	$ 3	$ 5	$ 6	$ 6
15,800	16,100	3	7	9	11	13
16,100	16,400	4	10	14	17	19
16,400	16,700	6	13	18	22	26
16,700	17,000	7	16	23	28	31
17,000	17,500	9	20	29	35	40
17,500	18,000	11	25	37	44	50
18,000	18,500	14	30	44	53	61
18,500	19,000	16	35	52	62	72
19,000	19,500	18	40	60	71	82
19,500	20,000	21	45	67	80	93
20,000	20,500	23	50	75	89	103
20,500	21,000	25	56	82	98	114
21,000	21,500	28	60	90	108	123
21,500	22,000	30	66	97	117	134
22,000	23,000	33	74	108	130	150
23,000	24,000	38	84	123	149	171
24,000	25,000	43	94	139	166	192
25,000	26,000	47	104	154	185	213
26,000	27,000	52	114	169	203	234
27,000	28,000	57	124	185	220	255
28,000	29,000	61	135	199	239	276

(Continued)

TABLE 6.3 *(Continued)*

Fair Market Value		Tax Year during Lease				
Over	Not Over	1st	2nd	3rd	4th	Later
29,000	30,000	66	145	214	258	296
30,000	31,000	71	155	230	275	318
31,000	32,000	75	165	245	294	338
32,000	33,000	80	175	260	312	360
33,000	34,000	85	185	276	329	381
34,000	35,000	89	196	290	348	402
35,000	36,000	94	206	305	367	422
36,000	37,000	99	216	321	384	443
37,000	38,000	103	226	336	403	464
38,000	39,000	108	236	351	421	485
39,000	40,000	112	247	366	439	506
40,000	41,000	117	257	381	457	527
41,000	42,000	122	267	396	475	549
42,000	43,000	126	278	411	493	570
43,000	44,000	131	288	426	512	590
44,000	45,000	136	298	441	530	611
45,000	46,000	140	308	457	548	632
46,000	47,000	145	318	472	566	653
47,000	48,000	150	328	487	584	674
48,000	49,000	154	339	502	602	695
49,000	50,000	159	349	517	620	717
50,000	51,000	164	359	532	639	737

TABLE 6.3 *(Continued)*

Fair Market Value		Tax Year during Lease				
Over	Not Over	1st	2nd	3rd	4th	Later
51,000	52,000	168	369	548	657	758
52,000	53,000	173	379	563	675	779
53,000	54,000	177	390	578	693	800
54,000	55,000	182	400	593	711	821
55,000	56,000	187	410	608	729	842
56,000	57,000	191	420	624	747	863
57,000	58,000	196	430	639	766	883
58,000	59,000	201	440	654	784	905
59,000	60,000	205	451	669	802	925
60,000	62,000	212	466	692	829	957
62,000	64,000	222	486	722	866	999
64,000	66,000	231	507	752	902	1,041
66,000	68,000	240	527	783	938	1,083
68,000	70,000	250	547	813	974	1,125
70,000	72,000	259	568	843	1,011	1,166
72,000	74,000	268	589	873	1,047	1,208
74,000	76,000	277	609	904	1,083	1,250
76,000	78,000	287	629	934	1,120	1,292
78,000	80,000	296	650	964	1,156	1,334
80,000	85,000	312	686	1,017	1,219	1,408
85,000	90,000	335	737	1,092	1,311	1,512
90,000	95,000	359	787	1,169	1,401	1,617

(Continued)

TABLE 6.3 *(Continued)*

Fair Market Value		Tax Year during Lease				
Over	Not Over	1st	2nd	3rd	4th	Later
95,000	100,000	382	838	1,245	1,491	1,722
100,000	110,000	417	915	1,358	1,627	1,880
110,000	120,000	463	1,017	1,509	1,810	2,089
120,000	130,000	510	1,119	1,660	1,991	2,299
130,000	140,000	556	1,221	1,812	2,172	2,509
140,000	150,000	603	1,323	1,963	2,354	2,718
150,000	160,000	649	1,425	2,115	2,535	2,928
160,000	170,000	696	1,527	2,266	2,717	3,137
170,000	180,000	742	1,629	2,418	2,898	3,347
180,000	190,000	789	1,731	2,569	3,080	3,556
190,000	200,000	835	1,833	2,720	3,262	3,766
200,000	210,000	881	1,935	2,872	3,443	3,976
210,000	220,000	928	2,037	3,023	3,625	4,185
220,000	230,000	974	2,139	3,175	3,806	4,395
230,000	240,000	1,021	2,241	3,326	3,988	4,604
240,000	250,000	1,067	2,343	3,478	4,169	4,814

For cars first leased *before* 2002, inclusion amounts for 2002 can be found in IRS Publication 463, "Travel, Entertainment, Gift, and Car Expenses," at www.irs.gov.

ELECTRIC CARS. A different table, also found in IRS Publication 463, is used to determine the inclusion amounts for electric cars first leased in 2002 that cost $46,000 or more.

Tax Credit for Electric Cars

If you buy a car powered primarily by electricity, you may be able to take a tax credit for its purchase. In 2002, the tax credit is 10 percent of the vehicle's cost or $4,000, whichever is less. The credit had been set to be reduced in 2002, but Congress extended the full credit through 2003.

LOOKING AHEAD

Starting in 2004, the tax credit for electric cars is reduced—by 25 percent in 2004, by 50 percent in 2005, and by 75 percent in 2006. No electric vehicle credit may be claimed in 2007 and later unless Congress extends the law.

Deduction for Gas-Electric Cars

Anyone—whether it's for business or personal purposes—may qualify to deduct up to $2,000 for the purchase of a clean-fuel car (different limits apply to trucks or vans weighing more than 10,000 pounds). The deduction is claimed "above-the-line" whether other deductions are itemized. This is a one-time deduction claimed in the year the car is purchased by an original owner (it can't be claimed for a used car). The IRS has now determined that clean-fuel cars include so-called hybrid cars powered by both gas and electricity (such as the Toyota Prius and the Honda Insight). These hybrid cars don't qualify for the credit for electric vehicles because they aren't power *entirely* by electricity.

The deduction relates only to the incremental cost of the clean fuel (electricity). Manufacturers must tell the IRS this amount and receive certification. A copy of this certification may be available to purchasers of these cars. To date, the

LOOKING AHEAD

The $2,000 limit for a clean-fuel car deduction is reduced by 25 percent in 2004, 50 percent in 2005, and 75 percent in 2006. Ford anticipates its 2004 Escape will be eligible for the reduced deduction, and General Motors expects a qualified pickup truck to be out in 2005. No deduction is permitted after 2006 unless Congress again extends the law.

IRS has certified the Toyota Prius, model years 2001, 2002, and 2003; the Honda Civic Hybrid, model year 2003; and the Honda Insight, model years 2000, 2001, and 2002. *Refund opportunity:* If you are entitled to the deduction for 2001, consider filing an amended return to claim it.

No deduction is allowed for the portion of the car taken into account for purposes of first-year expensing (discussed earlier in this chapter).

If the car is purchased for personal purposes, the deduction is claimed as an adjustment to gross income (i.e., you can deduct this amount even if you don't itemize your other deductions).

Other Travel and Entertainment Expenses

Substantiation Rules

Substantiation rules for travel and entertainment expenses are quite specific and must be followed in order to deduct these costs. Substantiation rules may be found in IRS Publication 463, "Travel, Entertainment, Gift, and Car Expenses," at www.irs.gov. The general rules have not changed for 2002.

ESTIMATIONS. The IRS and the U.S. Tax Court have made it clear that you can't estimate or extrapolate expenses and then deduct them. (See Examples 8 and 9.)

HIGH-LOW SUBSTANTIATION RATES. Instead of deducting the actual cost of lodging, meals, and incidental travel expenses, employees can substantiate business travel using a special high-low substantiation method. This method provides standard rates for travel to specific locations: The locations are either high-cost areas or not.

Effective on October 1, 2002, new rates take effect for the fiscal year ending September 30, 2003. At the time this book went to press, the new rates had not yet been announced

---

Example 8

You must keep a record of the miles you drive your personal car for business. This includes keeping track of the odometer. The U.S. Tax Court refused to allow a deduction for business mileage based on atlas readings of mileage between locations.

Example 9

You cannot take a sample of employee entertainment and meal costs and then extrapolate to the entire workforce to determine your deduction. The IRS insists on actual substantiation of each entertainment and meal expense incurred—even though this may impose a high administrative burden on an employer.

(you can find the new rates posted at www.policyworks.gov). You may elect to use the rates that became effective on October 1, 2001, for the final quarter of 2002. The rate for high-cost areas is $204 per day, and the rate for all other areas is $125 per day. Alternatively, you may use the old rates through September 30, 2002, and the new rates for the final quarter of 2002.

Frequent Flier Miles

If you receive frequent flier miles for business travel, you aren't taxed on this benefit, even if you use the mileage for personal travel. The IRS has given up on attempts to tax this benefit.

However, if you convert the mileage to cash, it is treated as taxable compensation to you.

Incentives for Hiring New Employees

If you own a business and have people work for you, the tax law encourages the hiring of certain workers by allowing you to take a tax credit for a portion of their wages. The type of credit depends on who you hire and where your business is located.

Work Opportunity Credit

The work opportunity credit is designed to encourage the employment of workers from certain targeted groups, such as former felons and those who are economically disadvantaged. The credit is generally up to 40 percent of a targeted employee's first-year wages, up to $6,000 for those who work at least 400 hours.

NEW CATEGORY OF ELIGIBLE WORKERS. The work opportunity credit can now be claimed for workers who qualify as "Liberty Zone taxpayers." These are individuals who substantially perform all of their services in the Liberty Zone and individuals who substantially perform all of their services in New York City for a business relocated from the Liberty Zone to someplace else within New York City because of the September 11 terrorist attacks.

The work opportunity credit, which had expired at the end of 2001, has been extended for two more years (through December 31, 2003).

Welfare-to-Work Credit

The welfare-to-work credit is designed to encourage the employment of long-term family assistance recipients. The credit is 35 percent of the first $10,000 of eligible wages in the first year of employment, plus 50 percent of the first $10,000 of eligible wages in the second year of employment, for a total credit of $8,500 per eligible employee.

Like the work opportunity credit, the welfare-to-work credit, which had expired at the end of 2001, has been extended for two more years (through December 31, 2003).

Caution

At the time this book went to press Congress was considering a measure to blend the work opportunity credit with the welfare-to-work credit. The law change would also simplify the certification process to ensure that workers fall within the categories that make employers eligible to claim the credit. Stay alert to possible law changes for 2002 or later.

Empowerment Zone Employment Credit

A special tax credit may be claimed for wages paid by a business within a designated empowerment zone to someone who lives and works within the zone. This special credit, called an empowerment zone employment credit, applies only to wages paid after 2001 (that is, for wages paid starting in 2002). The credit is 20 percent of the first $15,000 of qualified wages paid to full-time or part-time eligible employees. (See Example 10.)

Example 10

Your business is located within an empowerment zone. In 2002 you hire a new employee who earns $18,000 during the year. The employee lives and works within the zone. You may claim an empowerment zone employment credit of $3,000 (20 percent of wages up to $15,000).

Tax Write-offs for Medical Expenses

The tax law recognizes the ever-increasing cost of health care coverage and the burden this places on companies and self-employed individuals. To alleviate some of this burden, targeted write-offs apply.

Deduction for Self-Employed Individuals

Self-employed individuals, including sole proprietors, partners, LLC members, and more than 2 percent S corporation shareholders, cannot deduct health insurance from their business income. They can, however, deduct a percentage of their cost as an adjustment to gross income on Form 1040 (the deduction can be claimed even if they don't itemize other personal deductions). For 2002, the percentage is 70 percent of the premiums (up from 60 percent in 2001).

LOOKING AHEAD

The percentage of health insurance cost deductible by self-employeds from gross income increases in 2003 to 100 percent of the premiums. Stay alert for possible changes to the deduction. There have been proposals to allow the deduction to reduce business income for purposes of figuring self-employment tax paid by self-employed business owners.

Archer Medical Savings Accounts

Small businesses (those with 50 or fewer employees) and self-employed individuals can cope with their medical expenses on a tax-advantaged basis if they carry a high-deductible insurance policy and save for uncovered expenses through a special savings account. Contributions to the savings account are tax deductible and the account builds up on a tax-deferred basis. Funds can be tapped at any time to pay medical expenses not covered by insurance; withdrawals for this purpose are tax free. Withdrawals for any other purpose are taxable and subject to a 15 percent penalty. The penalty is waived for withdrawals starting at age 65. This arrangement of a high-deductible insurance policy combined with a special savings account is collectively referred to as an Archer medical savings account (MSA).

LIMITS ON DEDUCTIBLES AND OUT-OF-POCKET EXPENSES. In order to qualify for tax-deductible contributions to Archer MSAs, the insurance deductibles and out-of-pocket limitations under the medical policy must fall within set parameters. Due to cost-of-living adjustments, these parameters for 2002 are in Table 6.4.

As long as the insurance policy conforms to these limits, then tax-deductible contributions to a special savings account can be up to 65 percent of the policy's deductible for self-only coverage or 75 percent for family coverage. (See Example 11.)

TABLE 6.4 Limits for Archer MSAs

Type of Coverage	Limits on Policy Deductibles	Limit on Out-of-Pocket Expenses
Self-only	$1,650 to $2,500	$3,300
Family	$3,330 to $4,950	$6,050

Example 11

In 2002, a self-employed individual carries a policy for her family with a deductible of $4,500 and a limit on out-of-pocket expenses of $6,000. She may contribute up to $3,375 (75 percent of $4,500) to an Archer MSA.

An employer can make these deductible contributions. Alternatively, if the employer provides the high-deductible policy, employees can make their own deductible contributions.

Health Reimbursement Arrangements (HRAs)

The IRS had endorsed another type of arrangement that any employer—small or large—can use to enable employees to pay for medical costs with employer-funded contributions. An employer uses a high-deductible health insurance policy to keep premium costs low (this coverage can be paid by the employer, the employee,

LOOKING AHEAD

Archer medical savings accounts had been set to expire at the end of 2002. They have been given another one-year reprieve—through December 31, 2003. Any business or self-employed individual who starts an Archer MSA before the expiration date can continue to fund it even if the law is not extended once again. The limits on deductibles and out-of-pocket expenses will be adjusted for inflation in 2003.

At present, these medical arrangements have not been very popular. In some states it is difficult to find an insurer willing to write a high-deductible policy and provide a savings mechanism as well. However, interest is starting to grow, due in part to the continuing escalation in health insurance costs. It remains to be seen whether Congress again extends this tax break or changes it as has been proposed.

or a combination of both). Then an employer supplements the coverage through a health reimbursement arrangement (HRA) by contributing a fixed dollar amount for each employee with health coverage (such as $1,000 per year, but there's no dollar limit on employer contributions). The employer deducts contributions to the plan, and employees enjoy tax-free reimbursement of substantiated medical costs not covered by insurance. (Eligible medical expenses covered by the HRA do *not* include long-term care expenses.)

Any amounts contributed to the plan on an employee's behalf that aren't used within the year can carry over to later years (but no funds can be withdrawn for any reason other than the payment of medical expenses). For example, if the reimbursement limit for 2002 is fixed at $1,000 and the employee uses only $700, the reimbursement limit for 2003 becomes $1,300 ($1,000 annual contribution amount plus $300 carryover).

An HRA is treated as a group health plan subject to COBRA continuation requirements, so if you leave your job and the company is subject to COBRA, you can opt to continue benefits under the HRA. Former employees and retirees can continue to access their HRA accounts until funds are used up.

Caution

Self-employed individuals may not use HRAs to cover their out-of-pocket medical expenses.

Other Tax Changes

There are dozens of other tax changes affecting businesses. Here are some that have general applicability (that is, they aren't limited to a certain industry, such as insurance).

Net Operating Loss Carryback

Generally, net operating losses (NOLs) can be carried back for two years and forward for up to 20 years until they are fully used up. However, for NOLs arising in 2002, there is a longer carryback period of five years. (See Example 12.)

The longer carryback period is *only* for NOLs arising in 2001 or 2002. The reason for the longer carryback period is to give you an opportunity to utilize current losses to obtain tax refunds which, in turn, can be used to infuse cash into your business.

You are not required to use the longer carryback period. You can forgo it in favor of the usual two-year period. Alternatively, you can forgo any carryback entirely so that NOLs are only carried forward to future years. The election to forgo the carryback is irrevocable; you cannot change your mind later on to use a carryback, even if a subsequent audit

Example 12

In 2002, your business suffers a net operating loss. You may carry back the loss to 1997, then to 1998, 1999, 2000, and 2001.

of your return changes the income on which you based your decision to forgo the carryback in the first place.

PLANNING. It is generally advisable to forgo the carryback if you expect to be in a higher tax bracket in the coming years than you were in the carryback years. This will make your NOL carryovers worth more, as they'll be used to offset income that would otherwise be taxed at a higher rate, saving you more in taxes.

REFUND OPPORTUNITY. The IRS has provided guidance on how to claim the carryback to obtain a quick refund (or elect to forgo the longer carryback period). Taxpayers can obtain a quick refund for the longer carryback period generated by a 2001 NOL by filing the applicable form no later than October 31, 2002.

- Individuals (sole proprietors and owners of pass-through entities: File Form 1040X, Amended U.S. Individual Income Tax Return. Remember that owners of pass-through entities can each make separate elections with respect to NOLs generated by their share of the business losses.
- C corporations: File Form 1120X, Amended U.S. Corporation Income Tax Return, or Form 1129, Corporation Application for Tentative Refund.

ALTERNATIVE MINIMUM TAX. The carryback used for regular tax purposes applies for AMT purposes as well. For instance, if you use the five-year carryback for regular tax purposes, the same five-year carryback applies for AMT purposes.

For 2002, net operating losses can be used to offset 100 percent of alternative minimum taxable income. The 100 percent deduction applies only to NOLs arising in 2001 and 2002. More specifically, in figuring your NOL deduction for AMT purposes, it is the sum of ordinary NOLs subject to the 90 percent limit plus 2001 and 2002 NOLs subject to the 100 percent limit.

Liberty Zone Incentives

In addition to the added first-year expensing, bonus depreciation, and the new worker category for the work opportunity credit, there are other tax incentives for businesses affected by the September 11 terrorist attacks.

REPLACEMENT OF DESTROYED PROPERTY. When property is destroyed (or condemned) and gain results because insurance proceeds or other compensation exceed the adjusted basis of the property, such gain need not be currently recognized. The gain can be deferred if replacement property is acquired within set time limits. Gain on involuntarily converted property from the September 11 terrorist attacks can be deferred if qualified replacement property is acquired within a five-year replacement period. This five-year replacement period is instead of the usual two-year period. The only catch for the longer replacement period is that the replaced property must be substantially used within New York City.

LEASEHOLD IMPROVEMENTS. Generally, improvements made to leased property must be depreciated over the life of the property. For example, if improvements are made to commercial property, they must be depreciated over 39 years. However, for purposes of qualified New York City leasehold improvements, the recovery period is only five years, regardless of the recovery period for the underlying building. This shorter recovery period applies to leasehold improvements in a building located within the Liberty Zone that were put into service after September 10, 2001, and before January 1, 2007.

Credit for Starting a Retirement Plan

Small businesses (those with 100 or fewer employees) that have not yet set up qualified retirement plans, including 401(k) plans, simplified employee pension (SEP) plans, and SIMPLE plans, are encouraged to do so by means of tax incentives. Not only can the business deduct contributions on behalf of workers (within set limits); it can now claim a credit for the administrative costs of setting up the plan.

Starting in 2002, the credit is 50 percent of costs up to $1,000 (top credit is $500 per year). The credit may be claimed for the first three years of the plan, starting with the initial year of the plan. Any expenses not covered by the credit (including the other 50 percent of the first $1,000 of expenses used for figuring the credit) may be deducted as ordinary and necessary business expenses. (See Example 13.)

Example 13

In 2002, Company D sets up a 401(k) plan to cover its 20 employees. It incurs administrative and other start-up expenses for the plan of $6,400 in 2002, $5,600 in 2003, and $4,500 in 2004. Company D may claim a tax credit of $500 in 2002, 2003, and again in 2004. It may deduct $5,900 in 2002, $5,100 in 2003, and $4,000 in 2004.

The credit may *not* be claimed unless the plan covers at least one non-highly compensated employee. Thus, for example, a self-employed individual with no employees who first sets up a plan in 2002 cannot qualify for the credit.

PLANNING. You may opt to claim the credit in the year before the first year the plan is effective. However, no credit may be claimed for any year before 2002. (See Example 14.)

You are not *required* to claim the credit, even if you're eligible to do so. You may opt out of the credit to allow you to merely deduct the expenses.

Example 14

Same facts as in Example 13 except that the plan is started in 2003 (instead of 2002). In this case, Company D may opt to claim the credit in 2002 (the year preceding the first year in which the plan is effective).

Credit for Child Care Facilities

Many large companies already provide child care facilities for their employees in recognition of the fact that women are in the workforce in ever-increasing numbers. Now small and midsize companies are encouraged by the tax law to set up child care facilities for their employees. Doing so entitles a company to claim a new tax credit of 25 percent of qualified child care expenses plus 10 percent of qualified child care resources and referral expenditures. The credit may not exceed $150,000 in any year.

Qualified child care expenses are those incurred to buy, build, or rehabilitate a facility used for care of employees' children. This may be an on-site or off-site facility. The basis of any child care facility must be reduced by any expense taken into account in figuring the credit so that no double benefit may be claimed.

Qualified resource and referral expenditures include costs paid for referral services as long as they are provided to employees on a nondiscriminatory basis.

LOOKING AHEAD

If a business claims a credit for a child care facility and then ceases to use it for child care within 10 years, there is a recapture of the credit. The percentage of the credit is scaled down with the length of time the facility has been in operation.

Electronic Reporting of Form 1099s

If you pay independent contractors more than $600 in 2002, you must report such payments to them on Form 1099-

MISC no later than January 31, 2003. For the first time, however, you can opt to report the payments electronically if the recipient consents to this type of information return. Presumably, recipients can consent by e-mail to receive their information return electronically (this is the same method used by workers who consent to receive their W-2 forms electronically).

You have already been allowed to report the payments to the IRS electronically, so using this reporting method for recipients can simplify the process and save your business time and money.

OTHER ELECTRONIC REPORTING. Furnishing required information returns electronically is not limited to Form 1099-MISC. It can also be used for a variety of other information returns such as the following:

- Cash payments over $10,000 received in a trade or business reported on Form 8300.
- Exchanges of certain partnership interests reported on Form 8308.
- Dispositions of donated property reported on Form 8282.

CHAPTER 7

Miscellaneous Tax Changes

Some tax changes don't fit neatly into any of the categories discussed throughout this book. Still, these other changes may provide you with important tax-saving opportunities—or cost you extra taxes—for 2002.

This chapter covers a variety of tax rules that have changed for 2002 as a result of new laws or cost-of-living adjustments. These rules extend beyond income taxes, applying to certain excise and employment taxes you may be subject to.

Standard Deduction Amounts

Dollar Amounts

If you do not itemize your personal deductions, you instead claim a standard deduction amount. The dollar amounts of the standard deduction amount for your filing status have increased for 2002, as shown in Table 7.1.

ADDITIONAL STANDARD DEDUCTION AMOUNTS. Those age 65 and older and/or blind can claim an additional standard deduction amount if they don't itemize their deductions. For 2002, the additional standard deduction amount for singles is $1,150 ($900 for those who are married filing jointly or surviving spouses).

STANDARD DEDUCTION FOR DEPENDENTS. The standard deduction for dependents is essentially unchanged for 2002. It remains at the greater of $750 or the sum of $250 plus earned income, but cannot exceed the regular standard deduction of $4,700 for singles.

Strategies for Benefiting from Standard Deduction Increases

If your itemized expenses annually approximate your standard deduction amount, consider bunching your discretionary expenses so that you itemize in one year (when

TABLE 7.1 Standard Deductions

Filing Status	Standard Deduction
Single	$4,700
Head of household	6,900
Married filing jointly and surviving spouse	7,850
Married filing separately	3,925

your expenses exceed the standard deduction amount) and claim the standard deduction in the following year. You can alternate this strategy from year to year. (See Example 1.)

LOOKING AHEAD

The standard deduction amounts will again be adjusted for inflation in 2003, so expect to see increases for all taxpayers.

Reduction of Itemized Deductions

High-income taxpayers lose a portion of certain itemized deductions. For 2002, the point at which you are considered a high-income taxpayer subject to this reduction in your itemized deductions has increased. *Note:* The same limit applies to singles as well as to married couples filing jointly. Table 7.2

Example 1

In 2002, you know that your state income taxes will be about $4,500. Assuming you are single, if you make charitable contributions exceeding $2,000 for the year, you'll be able to itemize deductions. So make contributions in 2002 that you would ordinarily make over two years (2002 and 2003) to benefit from itemizing in 2002. Then you can claim the standard deduction in the following year. In 2004, again consider boosting your charitable contributions so that your itemized expenses exceed the standard deduction amount at that time.

TABLE 7.2 Itemized Deduction Limitations

Filing Status	AGI Over—
Married filing separately	$ 78,650
All other taxpayers	$137,300

shows the point at which itemized deductions start to be reduced.

LOOKING AHEAD

The AGI threshold will be adjusted for inflation in 2003. The reduction in itemized deductions for high-income taxpayers is eliminated by 2010. The phaseout of this reduction starts in 2006.

The reduction generally is 3 percent of AGI over the applicable limit. *Note:* The limit on itemized deductions does not impact write-offs for medical expenses, investment interest, gambling losses, and casualty and theft deductions.

Medical Expenses

Long-Term Care

The tax law recognizes the extraordinarily high cost of long-term care. Currently, the average annual cost of a nursing home is about $54,000 (and over $100,000 in some parts of the country). However, if you carry long-term care insurance to cover this cost, you may be able to achieve some tax benefit.

DEDUCTION FOR LONG-TERM CARE PREMIUMS. A portion of the annual cost of long-term care insurance is treated as a deductible medical expense. The dollar limits on premiums taken into account as medical expenses have increased for 2002, as shown in Table 7.3. (See also Example 2.)

Caution

Self-employed individuals who pay the cost of long-term care insurance can deduct 70 percent of the portion of such cost otherwise deductible in 2002 as an adjustment to gross income (up from 60 percent in 2001). The balance (30 percent) can be treated as an itemized medical expense, deductible to the extent that total medical costs exceed 7.5 percent of adjusted gross income.

EXCLUSION FOR BENEFITS PAID FROM LONG-TERM CARE POLICIES. Payments from long-term care policies are excludable to the extent they cover long-term care costs. If you receive a

TABLE 7.3 Dollar Limits for Long-Term Care Premiums

Your Age by Year-End	Deductible Portion of Long-Term Care Premiums
40 or less	$ 240
41 to 50	450
51 to 60	900
61 to 70	2,390
Over 70	2,990

Example 2

In 2002 when you're 65 years old, your annual premium for a long-term care policy is $2,600. You may include $2,390 as a medical expense along with your other deductible medical expenses. The total of your medical expenses is deductible to the extent it exceeds 7.5 percent of your AGI.

daily dollar payment without regard to costs, your exclusion is limited to $210 per day (up from $200 in 2001).

This same daily dollar limit applies to accelerated death benefits paid from a life insurance policy to an insured who is chronically ill (there is no limit on payments to an insured who is terminally ill).

LOANS TO CONTINUING CARE FACILITIES. If you pay a large entry fee to a continuing care facility that is refundable, it may be viewed as an interest-free loan that generates "interest income" to you—the amount that you should have charged under the below market interest rules based on the applicable federal rate of interest. However, loans up to a certain dollar amount are exempt from the below market interest rules. For 2002 this amount is $148,800 (up from $144,111 in 2001).

This exemption from the interest-free loan rules applies only if you or your spouse is at least age 65 by the end of the year and the continuing care contract provides you with a separate living unit, meals, and routine medical care, as well as skilled nursing home care at no additional substantial charge if such care becomes necessary.

Medical Transportation

If you travel to and from the doctor's office, pharmacy, or physical therapist, you can deduct your transportation costs. If you ride public transportation or take a taxi, you can deduct your actual out-of-pocket costs. If you use your car for this purpose, you don't have to figure your actual expenses—instead you can deduct a standard mileage rate. For 2002 the standard mileage rate for medical travel is 13 cents per mile (up from 12 cents per mile in 2001).

LOOKING AHEAD

In 2003, the dollar limits on annual long-term care insurance treated as deductible medical expenses will again be increased for inflation. Also, self-employed individuals will be able to deduct 100 percent of the portion of long-term care insurance related to their age as an adjustment to gross income. Finally, the nursing home loan amount will also be adjusted for inflation.

Caution

In order to deduct your medical travel costs you must keep records on the miles you drive for this purpose.

Weight Loss Programs

The cost of a weight loss program for someone diagnosed with obesity is fully deductible. However, the cost of special foods for someone who is obese and the cost of weight loss programs simply to maintain general good health or for cosmetic purposes are not deductible.

Surgery to remove loose skin following substantial weight loss is also a deductible medical expense (and not treated as nondeductible cosmetic surgery). The reason: The surgery also relates to the disease of obesity.

Health Insurance Credit

Under the Trade Act of 2002, if you are a "dislocated worker" (someone who loses his or her job because of obsolescence or foreign trade competition) or an uninsured retiree age 55 or older who has been dislocated and is receiving a pension from the Pension Benefit Guaranty Corporation (PBGC), you can claim a new tax credit to keep your health insurance coverage. For an eligible worker, the credit is up to 65 percent of the premium cost with no dollar limit.

The credit must be used either to continue COBRA coverage through an employer's policy or to purchase insurance in state-run health care arrangements, generally administered for state employees. You cannot use the funds to purchase an individual policy unless it was purchased one month before losing your job.

The credit, which starts in December 2002, is refundable (i.e., it can be claimed even if it exceeds your tax liability), although it is not expected that a refundable mechanism will be in place until some time in 2003.

Other Medical Expense Changes

Changes to business-related medical expenses, including a discussion of Archer medical savings accounts and the adjustments-to-gross-income deduction for health insurance of self-employed individuals, are discussed in Chapter 6.

Moving Expenses

If you make a job-related move that meets time and distance tests, you can deduct your out-of-pocket costs as a deduction from gross income. For purposes of this deduction, if you use your car to move household goods and/or your family, you can deduct your related expenses. Instead of figuring your actual costs you can deduct a standard mileage rate. For 2002 the standard mileage rate for move-related travel is 13 cents per mile (up from 12 cents per mile in 2001).

Transportation Fringe Benefits

Employer-paid transportation fringe benefits can be received tax free by most employees. The dollar limit for these benefits is expressed as monthly amounts, which have been increased for 2002. The limits are stated in Table 7.4.

If you receive a benefit in excess of this dollar limit (for

TABLE 7.4 Transportation Fringe Benefits

Type of Transportation Benefit	Monthly Dollar Limit
Free parking	$185
Transit passes*	100
Van pooling*	100

*The monthly dollar limit is a combined amount if you receive both types of benefits.

LOOKING AHEAD

The dollar limits on these transportation fringe benefits may be adjusted for inflation after 2002.

example, monthly parking valued at $200 per month), only the excess is taxable.

Note: Partners, LLC members, more than 2 percent S corporation shareholders, and independent contractors can receive transit passes and van pooling worth up to $21 per month; if the benefit's value is more, then the entire benefit is taxable. These individuals cannot receive commuter parking benefits tax free unless the benefits are *de minimis*.

Home Sales

If you sell your home, you may be able to avoid tax on your profit. The law allows you to exclude up to $250,000 of gain ($500,000 on a joint return) if you owned and used your home for two out of five years before the date of sale.

But what happens if you're forced to sell before satisfying the two-year period? The law allows you to prorate the exclusion for the period of use if the sale results from a change in employment or health or unforeseen circumstances. (See Example 3.)

At the time this book went to press, regulations defining the term "unforeseen circumstances" were to be released shortly. Expected to be included in the regulations are the following situations:

- Divorce (or breakup of a permanent relationship among the home's co-owners).

Example 3

You're single and bought your home in July 2001 for $260,000. You lost your job as a result of the September 11 terrorist attack and were unable to find a new job quickly, forcing you to sell your home in July 2002 (after only one year) for $290,000. You can fully exclude your gain of $30,000 ($290,000 – $260,000) since it is less than your exclusion, which is limited to $125,000 (half the $250,000 maximum exclusion).

- Unemployment (e.g., being fired and unable to find a new position.
- Relocation because of safety or nuisance.
- Caring for a sick parent or other relative.
- Relocation of military personnel.

REFUND OPPORTUNITY. If you failed to claim an exclusion for a sale prior to 2002 because you weren't sure you were eligible to claim it, you can consider filing an amended return to obtain a tax refund. Use Form 1040X, Amended U.S. Individual Income Tax Return, for this purpose.

Alert: At the time this book went to press, Congress was considering special breaks for military personnel. One provision would ease eligibility requirements for the home-sale exclusion. Eligible members of the uniformed armed services would be allowed to exclude the duration of an extended deployment from the five-year calculation. To be eligible, personnel must be deployed more than 250 miles away from their residence (or under orders to remain in government facilities) and the assignment must last more than 180 days or be open-ended. If the election is made, the five-year period is figured without taking into account any period (up to five years) during which the taxpayer or the taxpayer's spouse is on qualified official extended duty. This change would apply to periods after the law becomes effective.

Foreign Earned Income Limit

LOOKING AHEAD

The $80,000 foreign earned income exclusion limit will not increase next year. However, starting in 2006, the limit will be adjusted annually for inflation in increments of $100.

If you live and work abroad, you are still subject to U.S. income taxes. However, you may be eligible to exclude your foreign earnings from income (up to a set dollar limit). For 2002, the foreign earned income exclusion limit increased to $80,000 (up from $78,000 in 2001).

Estimated Taxes

You must pay your tax liability for the year throughout the year—through withholding on wages or certain other payments—or by making installments of your tax payments. The amount of your payments should be sufficient to avoid underpayment penalties.

Estimated Taxes

For 2002, your estimated taxes—through withholding, estimated tax payments, or a combination of both—to avoid penalty must be at least 90 percent of the tax due for 2002 or 100 percent of the tax shown on your 2001 return, whichever is less.

The 100 percent safe harbor cannot be used if you are considered a "high-income taxpayer." You fall into this category if in 2001 your adjusted gross income exceeded $150,000 ($75,000 if you were married and filed a separate return). In this case, the prior year safe harbor means paying 112 percent of your 2001 liability. (See Examples 4 and 5.)

LOOKING AHEAD

Starting in 2003, the 100 percent safe harbor for high-income taxpayers drops to 110 percent of 2002 tax liability. This safe harbor will remain constant in future years. In other words, anytime you find yourself classified as a high-income taxpayer, you'll have to pay at least 110 percent of your prior year's tax liability in the current year to avoid estimated tax penalties if you don't pay at least 90 percent of your current year liability.

Withholding

The withholding tables on your wages will change again in 2003 to reflect cost-of-living adjustments to the tax brack-

Example 4

In 2001 your adjusted gross income was $85,000 and your tax liability was $14,000. In 2002 your income increased and you anticipate owing $20,000. To avoid estimated tax penalties for 2002, your payments through withholding and estimated taxes must be at least $14,000 (100 percent of last year's tax liability) since this is less than $18,000 (90 percent of 2002 tax liability).

Example 5

Your adjusted gross income in 2001 was $160,000, your tax liability was $40,000, and your 2002 liability is expected to be $50,000. In this instance, since you are considered a high-income taxpayer, you must pay through withholding and estimated tax at least $44,800 (112 percent of $40,000), since this is less than $45,000 (90 percent of $50,000).

ets. If you want to change your withholding allowances—to have more or less withheld from your pay—you must file a new Form W-4 with your employer. Otherwise the employer will figure your withholding in 2003 based on whatever allowances you claimed in 2002.

Excise Tax on Luxury Cars

New passenger cars costing more than a fixed dollar amount (including any after-market accessories installed within six months of purchase) are subject to a luxury tax upon purchase. For 2002, the excise tax rate has declined and the dollar amount used for determining a luxury car has increased—reducing the tax and exempting more cars from it.

In 2002, the excise tax rate on a luxury car is 3 percent (down from 4 percent in 2001). A luxury car is one costing

LOOKING AHEAD

The excise tax on luxury cars is set to expire at the end of 2002 unless Congress takes further action. It may be continued as a source of needed revenue for the federal government.

more than $40,000 (up from $38,000 in 2001) on the car's first retail purchase.

FICA, Self-Employment Tax, and Social Security Benefits

FICA

The tax rates on the Social Security and Medicare portions of FICA tax for employers and employees remain unchanged for 2002. The Social Security tax rate is 6.2 percent and the Medicare tax rate is 1.45 percent.

However, the wage base limit on which the Social Security portion of the tax is figured is limited to $84,900 (up from $80,400 in 2001). There is no wage base limit for the Medicare portion of the tax. (See Example 6.)

Self-Employment Tax

Self-employed individuals pay the employer and employee share of FICA. Thus, they pay a Social Security tax rate of 12.4 percent and a Medicare tax rate of 2.9 percent. One-half of this tax is deductible as an adjustment to gross income.

Example 6

In 2002, you receive a salary of $85,000 from XYZ Corp. You pay $5,263.80 in Social Security tax ($84,900 × 6.2%) and $1,232.50 in Medicare tax ($85,000 × 1.45%) for a total FICA payment of $6,496.30.

LOOKING AHEAD

The wage base limit for the Social Security portion of FICA and self-employment tax is set to increase. Current projections put that figure in excess of $90,000.

The basis on which the Social Security portion of the self-employment tax is figured—net earnings from self-employment—also is set at $84,900 (up from $80,400 in 2001). As in the case of FICA, there is no limit on net earnings from self-employment for the Medicare portion of self-employment tax.

Social Security Benefits

LOOKING AHEAD

Note that the age 65 threshold at which point Social Security benefits are not reduced regardless of earnings remains constant even though the normal retirement age when the full benefit rate is payable starts to increase in 2003. Thus, someone born in 1938 has a normal retirement age of 65 years, two months, which is attained in 2003 (or 2004 if born in November or December 1938). Still, as long as benefits do not start before one's 65th birthday, there is no reduction of Social Security benefits on account of excess earnings.

Recipients under the age of 65 lose a portion of their Social Security benefits (besides their benefit rate being reduced by a certain percentage for each month they were under retirement age when the benefit began) if earnings from a job or self-employment exceed a set dollar amount. For 2002, that dollar limit is fixed at $11,280 (up from $10,680 in 2001). For every two dollars of excess earnings, benefits are reduced by one dollar.

Those over the age of 65 do not have any reduction in benefits, regardless of their earn-

> **Caution**
>
> You continue to pay Social Security taxes on your earnings from a job or self-employment, regardless of age—even if you are collecting benefits.

ings. However, in the year of the 65th birthday, benefits can be reduced if earnings *before* that date exceed a set amount. The monthly limit for 2002 is $2,500 (up from $2,084 in 2001). For every three dollars of excess earnings, benefits are reduced by one dollar.

Government-Paid Attorneys' Fees

If you successfully contest an IRS action against you in an administrative proceeding or in court, you may be able to recover your attorneys' fees and other costs from the federal government. To recover, you must meet *all* of the following requirements:

- You exhausted your IRS administrative remedies and did not unreasonably delay any proceedings (i.e., you followed the audit process through all IRS appeals).
- You "substantially prevail"—you win your position in a court action or administrative proceeding (or you lose but the IRS obtains a judgment that is no more than the amount you offered in settlement)—*and* the IRS cannot show that it was "substantially justified" in pursuing its position.

- Your claim for attorneys' fees, court costs, and other related expenses is reasonable.

- You did *not* represent yourself (you cannot recover anything if you represent yourself, even if you are an attorney trying to recover your ordinary hourly fee for the time you expended in winning your position).

Recoveries for attorneys' fees generally are limited to a set dollar hourly rate. For 2002, this rate is fixed at $150 per hour (up from $140 per hour in 2001). *Note:* In rare cases you may be able to recover more if you can show special circumstances.

Free Electronic Tax Preparation and Filing

In the government's effort to encourage taxpayers to file their returns electronically using the IRS e-file system, a consortium of certain private tax software companies have agreed to provide free online tax preparation and filing opportunities for certain taxpayers. At the time this book went to press it was not yet clear which taxpayers would qualify for this free service. Last year a number of companies had already offered the free service to taxpayers with adjusted gross income below $25,000. Details of eligibility for this free service will be available at the IRS web site (www.irs.gov).

Appendix

State-by-State College Savings Plans

All plans accept accounts for both residents and nonresidents unless otherwise noted.

State	Fund Manager	Phone	Comment
Alabama			Under development
Alaska	T. Rowe Price	866-521-1894	
	T. Rowe Price and Manulife Financial	866-222-7498	Broker only (in and out of state)
Arizona	College Savings Bank	800-888-2723	
	Securities Management and Research	888-667-3239	

(Continued)

State	Fund Manager	Phone	Comment
Arkansas	Mercury Funds	877-442-6553	Broker only (out of state)
California	TIAA-CREF	877-728-4338	
Colorado	Salomon Smith Barney	800-478-5651 888-572-4652 (out of state)	
Connecticut	TIAA-CREF	888-779-CHET	
Delaware	Fidelity Investments	800-544-1655	
District of Columbia			Under development
Florida			Under development
Georgia	TIAA-CREF	877-424-4377	
Hawaii	Delaware Investments	808-643-4529 866-529-3343 (out of state)	
Idaho	TIAA-CREF	866-433-2533	
Illinois	Salomon Smith Barney		
Indiana	One Group Investments	866-400-7526	Broker only (in and out of state)
Iowa	State Treasurer and Vanguard	888-672-9116	
Kansas	American Century	800-579-2203	
Kentucky	TIAA-CREF	877-598-7878	Need Kentucky ties to contribute
Louisiana	State	800-259-5626	Louisiana residents only

State	Fund Manager	Phone	Comment
Maine	Merrill Lynch	877-463-9843	
Maryland	T. Rowe Price	888-463-4723	
Massachusetts	Fidelity Investments	800-544-2776	
Michigan	TIAA-CREF	877-861-MESP	
Minnesota	TIAA-CREF	877-338-4646	
Mississippi	TIAA-CREF	800-338-3670	
Missouri	TIAA-CREF	888-414-6678	
Montana	College Savings Bank	800-888-2723	
Nebraska	Union Bank and Trust	888-993-3746	
	Union Bank and AIM	877-246-7526	Broker only (in and out of state)
	TD Waterhouse	877-408-4644	
Nevada	Strong Capital Management and American Skandia	800-SKANDIA	Broker only (in and out of state)
	Strong Capital Management	877-529-5295	
New Hampshire	Fidelity Investments	800-522-7297 800-544-1722	Broker only (in and out of state)
New Jersey	State	877-4NJBEST	Residents only
New Mexico	Schoolhouse Capital	877-EDPLANS	
	Schoolhouse Capital and Oppenheim	866-529-7283	Broker only (in and out of state)

(Continued)

177

State	Fund Manager	Phone	Comment
New Mexico *(cont.)*	Schoolhouse Capital and New York Life Investment Management	866-529-7367	Broker only (in and out of state)
	Schoolhouse Capital	877-277-4838	Broker only (in and out of state)
New York	TIAA-CREF	877-697-2837	
North Carolina	College Foundation Inc.	800-600-3453	Residents and those employed in state
	College Foundation Inc. and J&W Seligman	800-600-3453	Broker only
North Dakota	Morgan Stanley	866-728-3529	Nonresidents starting mid-2002
Ohio	Putnam	800-AFFORD IT	Residents only
	Putnam	800-225-1518	Nonresidents only
Oklahoma	TIAA-CREF	877-654-7284	
Oregon	Strong Capital Management	866-772-8464	
Pennsylvania			Under development
Rhode Island	Alliance Capital	888-324-5057	Nonresidents through broker only
South Carolina	Banc of America Advisors LLC	800-244-5674 800-765-2668	Nonresidents through broker only
South Dakota	PIMCO Funds	866-529-7462	Nonresidents through broker only
Tennessee	TIAA-CREF	888-486-BEST	
Texas			Under development

State	Fund Manager	Phone	Comment
Utah	State agency	800-418-2551	
Vermont	TIAA-CREF	800-637-5860	
Virginia	Virginia College Savings Plan and American Funds	800-421-4120 888-567-0540	Broker only (in and out of state)
Washington			Under development
West Virginia	Hartford Life	866-574-3542	Nonresidents through broker only
Wisconsin	Strong Investments	888-338-3789 866-677-6933	Broker only (in and out of state)
Wyoming	Mercury Advisors	877-529-2655	Nonresidents through broker only

Glossary

above-the-line deductions   Items subtracted from gross income to arrive at adjusted gross income (AGI).

adjusted basis   The basis of property reduced by any allowable adjustments such as first-year expensing and depreciation.

adjusted gross income (AGI)   Gross income less allowable adjustments, such as deductions for IRA contributions, alimony payments, and one-half of self-employment tax. AGI determines eligibility for various tax benefits (e.g., certain itemized deductions, making IRA contributions if you're a plan participant, deducting $25,000 rental loss allowance, and converting a traditional IRA to a Roth IRA).

alternative minimum tax (AMT)   A tax triggered if certain tax benefits reduce your regular income tax below the tax computed on Form 6251 for AMT purposes.

Archer medical savings account (MSA)   A type of medical plan combining high-deductible medical insurance with an IRA-type savings account to pay unreimbursed medical expenses.

B

basis   Generally, the amount paid for property. You need to know your basis to figure gain or loss on a sale or, in the case of business or investment property, the depreciation that can be claimed.

bonus depreciation   An additional 30 percent depreciation allowance for the first year business property is placed in service after September 10, 2001, and before January 1, 2005.

C

capital gains rates Special tax rates imposed on sales or exchanges resulting in long-term capital gains.

carryback A tax technique for receiving a refund of taxes in prior years by applying a deduction or credit from a current year to a prior tax year. For example, a business net operating loss incurred in 2002 may be carried back for five years.

carryforward A tax technique of applying a loss or credit from a current year to a later tax year. For example, a business net operating loss incurred in 2002 may be carried forward for 20 years.

cash method of accounting Reporting income when actually or constructively received and deducting expenses when paid.

charitable organization Tax-exempt organization to which contributions can be made on a tax-deductible basis. Charitable organizations may *not* be treated as designated beneficiaries of IRAs or qualified retirement plan benefits.

child For tax purposes, different definitions apply for different purposes (with as many as five different definitions covered in this book).

child and dependent care credit A credit of up to 30 percent of certain care expenses incurred to allow you to work.

child tax credit A credit in 2002 of up to $600 per eligible child (under the age of 17) if your income does not exceed certain limits.

conservation easement A right given to a charitable organization or government body to use land for recreation, the preservation of open space, or plant or wildlife refuges.

constructive receipt A tax rule that taxes income that is not actually received by you but that you may draw upon.

continuing care facility A living arrangement that provides a separate living unit, meals, and routine medical expenses.

cost-of-living adjustment An increase in a tax item due to the rate of inflation.

Coverdell education savings account (ESA) A special savings account to fund certain education expenses (formerly called an education IRA).

credit An item that reduces tax liability on a dollar-for-dollar basis.

D

deductions   Items directly reducing income for tax purposes. Personal deductions, such as medical expenses, are allowed only if you itemize them on Schedule A. Other deductions, such as alimony and student loan interest, are subtracted from gross income (even if other deductions aren't itemized).

deemed sale   An election made on a tax return to treat assets owned at the start of that year to have been sold and reacquired in order to start a holding period for purposes of favorable capital gains rates.

deferred compensation   A portion of earnings withheld by an employer (or put into a retirement plan) for distribution to the employee at a later date. If certain requirements are met, the deferred amounts are not currently taxable but are taxed when received at that later time (typically retirement).

defined benefit plan   A retirement plan that pays fixed benefits based on actuarial projections.

defined contribution plan   A retirement plan that pays benefits based on contributions to individual accounts, plus accumulated earnings. Contributions generally are based on a percentage of salary or net earnings from self-employment.

dependency exemption A fixed deduction of $3,000 in 2002 that a taxpayer may claim for each qualifying dependent who may not be claimed as a dependent on another taxpayer's return. *See also* **personal exemptions.**

dependent A person supported by another person. If certain tests are met, a dependency exemption may be claimed for the dependent.

designated beneficiary A person (or trust) in existence on September 30 of the year following the death of an IRA owner or employee who is named in an IRA or qualified retirement plan to receive distributions.

disaster relief payments Tax-free payment to cover personal, family, living, or funeral expenses of a terrorist victim.

E

earned income Compensation for performing work. You must have earned income to make an IRA contribution or claim the earned income credit.

earned income credit (EIC) A tax credit allowed to a taxpayer with earned income (or AGI) below certain thresholds.

education credit A credit for paying certain qualified higher education costs. There are two types: the Hope credit and the lifetime learning credit.

educator For purposes of the tax deduction for educator expenses, educators are teachers, aides, counselors, and principals in grades K through 12 who work at least 900 hours during the school year.

elective deferrals A portion of an employee's salary withheld and contributed to a 401(k) or other retirement plan. These amounts are not currently taxed as salary.

estate tax A tax imposed on the value of a decedent's taxable estate, after deductions and credits.

estimated tax Advance payment of current tax liability based either on wage withholding or on installment payments of estimated tax liability. Payments must meet certain requirements to avoid underpayment penalty.

exemption For AMT purposes, an exemption it is an amount subtracted from alternative minimum taxable income. For estate, gift, and generation-skipping transfer tax purposes, it is an amount that is translated into a credit to offset the applicable tax. *See also* **dependency exemption; personal exemption.**

F

fair market value   What a willing buyer would pay to a willing seller when neither is under any compulsion to buy or sell.

fellowship   *See* **scholarship.**

first-year expensing   A deduction up to a set dollar limit for the cost of business equipment placed in service during the year. This deduction is also called a Section 179 deduction.

529 plan   *See* **qualified tuition plan.**

flexible spending arrangement (FSA)   A salary reduction plan that allows employees to pay for medical coverage or dependent care expenses on a pretax basis.

foreign child   A child who is not a U.S. citizen or resident at the time adoption efforts commence.

foreign earned income exclusion   In 2002, up to $80,000 of foreign earned income is exempt from tax if a foreign residence or physical presence test is met.

401(k) plan   A deferred pay plan authorized by Section 401(k) of the Internal Revenue Code under which a percentage of an employee's salary is withheld (called an elective deferral) and placed in a qualified retirement plan. Income on the elective deferrals accumulates on a tax-deferred basis until withdrawn by the employee (generally when retiring or leaving the company).

457 plan   A deferred compensation plan set up by a state or local government or tax-exempt organization that allows tax-free deferrals of salary.

G

generation-skipping transfer (GST) tax A tax on a transfer that skips a generation (e.g., from grandparent to grandchild) in excess of an exemption amount ($1.1 million in 2002).

gift tax   Gifts in 2002 in excess of $11,000 per donee annual exclusion are subject to gift tax, but the tax may be offset by a person's lifetime gift tax exemption amount.

gross income   The total amount of income received from all sources before exclusions and deductions.

H

head of household   Generally, an unmarried person who maintains a household for one or more dependents and is allowed to compute income tax based on head of household rates (which are more favorable than single person rates).

high-income taxpayers   Taxpayers with AGI over a set limit who are subject to certain phaseouts or reductions in benefits. They are also subject to a different estimated tax safe harbor.

home sale exclusion   A portion of gain on the sale of a main home that can be received tax free if certain conditions are met.

hybrid car   Car powered by both gas and electricity; hybrid cars are eligible for a special $2,000 deduction.

I

incentive stock option (ISOs)   Option meeting tax law tests that defer regular income tax on the option transaction until the obtained stock is sold (but the exercise of ISOs may give rise to AMT).

inclusion amount   In the case of cars leased for business, an amount that must be added back to income for cars that initially have a fair market value over a set dollar amount.

income shifting A tax technique designed to shift income among family members from one who is in a higher tax bracket to another in a lower tax bracket.

indexing *See* **cost-of-living adjustment.**

individual retirement account (IRA) A retirement account to which a limited contribution is permitted annually from earned income (or alimony), but tax deductions are restricted for active participants in qualified retirement plans who earn over set amounts.

installment sale A sale of property that allows for tax deferment if at least one payment is received after the year in which the sale occurs. The installment method does not apply to year-end sales of publicly traded securities. Dealers may not use the installment method. Investors with very large installment balances could face a special tax.

irrevocable trust Trust that cannot be changed by the creator once it comes into existence.

itemized deductions Items, such as medical expenses, home mortgage interest, and state and local taxes, that are claimed as write-offs on Schedule A of Form 1040 in lieu of claiming the standard deduction. Itemized deductions are subtracted from AGI to arrive at taxable income. The amount of itemized deductions is subject to a reduction when AGI exceeds certain limits.

J

joint return   A return filed by a married couple reporting their combined income and deductions. Joint return status generally provides tax savings over filing separate returns for married couples.

K

kiddie tax   The tax on investment income in excess of $1,500 in 2002 of a child under age 14, based on the parents' top marginal tax rate and computed on Form 8615.

L

Liberty Zone   Generally, the area in New York City below Canal Street that was affected by the September 11 terrorist attack.

long-term capital gain or loss   Gain or loss on the sale or exchange of a capital asset held more than one year.

luxury car   Car costing more than a certain amount; luxury cars are subject to dollar limits on depreciation, trigger inclusion amounts if leased, and result in excise taxes.

M

marital deduction   An estate and gift tax deduction for assets passing to a spouse. In the case of a spouse who is a U.S. citizen, it allows for completely tax-free transfers.

marriage penalty   The additional tax paid by a married couple that would not be owed if they had remained single.

miscellaneous itemized deductions   Generally, itemized deductions for job and investment expenses subject to a floor of 2 percent of AGI.

modified adjusted gross income (MAGI)   Generally, adjusted gross income increased by certain items (e.g., tax-free foreign earned income). MAGI is used to determine the phaseouts for certain deductions and credits.

moving expenses   Certain expenses of moving to a new job location are deductible if distance and time tests are met.

N

net operating loss (NOL)   A business loss that exceeds current income may be carried back against income of prior years and carried forward as a deduction from future income until eliminated.

O

ordinary income   Income other than capital gains.

ordinary loss   A loss other than a capital loss.

P

personal exemption   A deduction of $3,000 in 2002 that every taxpayer (other than someone who can be claimed as a dependent of another taxpayer) may claim for himself or herself, and for a spouse on a joint return. *See also* **dependency exemptions.**

placed in service   The time when a depreciable asset is ready to be used in business. The date fixes the beginning of the depreciation period or eligibility for first-year expensing.

probate estate   Property held in a decedent's name passing by will (or under the terms of state laws of intestacy).

profit-sharing plan   A defined contribution plan under which the amount contributed to employees' accounts is based on a percentage of the employer's profits.

Q

qualified plan   A retirement plan that meets tax law tests and allows tax deferment and tax-free accumulation of income until benefits are withdrawn. Pension, profit-sharing, SEP, and SIMPLE plans are qualified plans.

qualified tuition plan   A higher education savings plan sponsored by a state or private institution.

qualifying widow or widower   A filing status entitling the taxpayer with a dependent to use joint tax rates (and the standard deduction for joint filers) for up to two years after the death of a spouse.

R

refundable tax credit   A credit that entitles you to receive a refund even if the amount exceeds your tax for the year.

required minimum distribution (RMD)   Annual withdrawal from an IRA or a qualified plan designed to avoid a 50 percent penalty.

retirement savings contributions credit   A credit for elective deferrals or IRA contributions that may be claimed by a person with income below a set limit (in addition to any other tax benefit related to the elective deferrals or IRA contributions).

revocable trust A trust that may be changed or terminated by its creator (e.g., a living trust). Such trusts generally do not provide any income tax savings to the creator.

rollover A tax-free reinvestment of a distribution from a qualified retirement plan or IRA into another plan or IRA within 60 days.

Roth IRA A nondeductible IRA that allows for tax-free accumulations of earnings.

S

salary reduction agreement Consent to have an employer withhold a portion of wages that will be contributed to a qualified retirement plan or flexible spending arrangement. Such amounts are not currently taxed as wages.

salary reduction simplified employee pension (SARSEP) A retirement plan set up before 1997 that allows employees to make elective deferrals (i.e., contributions of a portion of wages) on a pretax basis.

savings incentive match plan for employees (SIMPLE) A type of retirement plan funded by elective deferrals and employer matching contributions.

scholarship Grant to a degree candidate that receives tax-free treatment if used for tuition and course-related expenses.

Section 179 deduction *See* **first-year expensing.**

self-employed person An individual who operates a business or profession as a proprietor or independent contractor and reports self-employment income on Schedule C.

self-employment tax Social Security and Medicare taxes paid by a self-employed person. The Social Security portion is 12.4 percent of net earnings from self-employment up to $84,900 in 2002. The Medicare portion is 2.9 percent of all net earnings from self-employment. One-half of the total self-employment tax is deductible.

separate returns Returns filed individually by married persons who do not file a joint return. Filing separately may save taxes where each spouse has separate deductions, but certain tax benefits require joint filing.

short-term capital gain or loss Gain or loss on the sale or exchange of a capital asset held one year or less.

simplified employee pension (SEP) plan An IRA-type plan set up by an employer or self-employed person rather than an employee.

single The filing status of a person who is unmarried on December 31 of the year for which a return is filed.

special needs child For purposes of a Coverdell ESA, this is someone who requires more time to complete his or her education because of a physical, mental, or emotional condition. For purposes of the adoption credit, this is a child under age 18 who is physically or mentally incapable of self-care.

standard deduction A fixed deduction allowed to those who do not itemize deductions. The amount depends on filing status, age, and whether a person is blind.

standard mileage rate A fixed rate set by the IRS for deducting auto expenses in lieu of deducting actual costs.

T

taxable income Net income after claiming all deductions (including personal exemptions).

tax bracket In 2002, there are six individual federal income tax brackets—10 percent, 15 percent, 27 percent, 30 percent, 35 percent, and 38.6 percent.

tax-free exchange A trade of property that defers the recognition of gain until the property received in the transaction is later disposed of (but only if qualified property is involved).

tax preference items   Items that may subject a taxpayer to the alternative minimum tax (AMT).

terrorist victim   Person injured or killed in or as a result of the Oklahoma bombing on April 19, 1995; the attacks on September 11, 2001; or anthrax incidents occurring after September 10, 2001, and before January 1, 2002.

trust   An arrangement under which one person transfers legal ownership of assets to another person or corporation (the trustee) for the benefit of one or more parties (beneficiaries).

U

unearned income   Investment income or other income that is *not* derived from performing work for pay.

V

vesting   The process of accruing an interest in contributions that are treated as earned. Employee contributions are always 100 percent vested. Employer contributions may be immediately vested or vested over a set schedule.

W

withholding An amount taken from income as a prepayment of tax liability for the year. In the case of wages, the employer withholds part of every wage payment for this purpose.

Index